HEY THERE, HIGH FLYER

Published in Canada, for Global Distribution
by YGTMedia Co. www.ygtmedia.co
For more information email: info@ygtmedia.co

ISBN trade paperback: 978-1-998754-62-5
eBook: 978-1-998754-63-2

To order additional copies of this book:
info@ygtmedia.co

HEY THERE, HIGH FLYER

The High-Achieving Woman's Guide to
Confidence & Self-Management

BARBARA MORRIS-BLAKE

To the incredible high-flying women whom I've had the privilege to coach—sharing your stories, triumphs, vulnerabilities, and fears have not only shaped this book but have inspired countless other women to rise above. Your journeys of tenacity and resilience are woven into this book.

To my husband, Jeff Heckler—I had dreamed of a love profound and true but never imagined it would come wrapped in a soul as remarkable as you. Your unwavering encouragement, belief, and love have shown me that I truly can achieve anything. Thank you for being my rock, my anchor, and my guiding star.

To my amazing children—Mick, Jon, and Tara—you've been my most insightful guides, revealing the resilience and balance that life can offer. Being your mom fills me with boundless gratitude, and although I wish I'd possessed the knowledge in these pages when you were younger, our shared journey has been a wellspring of joy and personal development. Let this book be a testament to the strength and wisdom you've imparted to me along the way.

This book honors the high-achieving women, the dreamers, and every determined female spirit who aspires to fly higher.

DISCLAIMER

The stories presented in this book are composite portrayals of clients and events crafted by the author for artistic and educational purposes. While inspired by real-life experiences, the author has taken great care to ensure that no identifying details or actual names have been used to protect the privacy and confidentiality of individuals.

Readers are advised that the content of this book is not to be construed as medical or psychological advice. The author is not a licensed doctor in any field depicted in this book. If you identify any area of your life that requires attention or treatment, please seek guidance from a medical professional.

TABLE OF CONTENTS

INTRODUCTION

I didn't start out as a high achiever. Growing up, all I wanted was a family—to own a home with a sliding glass door and no-wax floors. That was my lifelong goal—being a wife and mother, and like my mother, a wonderful homemaker. You may be sarcastically thinking, *Way to dream big, Barbara.* But that was *my* big dream.

And I got what I wanted. I married at twenty and had my first child at twenty-one. By the time I was thirty-one, I had three children. But as much as I loved being a mom, it wasn't enough. I had a drive that I couldn't ignore: the drive of a high achiever. Mastering a skill or reaching a goal only propelled me forward to learn new skills and set higher goals. As a wife, mother, and career woman, I felt driven to do it all. And I did.

Twenty years ago I took a big risk and started a consulting business that has pivoted when necessary and has continued to grow over the last two decades. As an executive coach, I have worked with hundreds of high achievers, and I see my younger self in many of them.

Both men and women fall prey to the pitfalls of being a high achiever, but this book is for women. Female high achievers have issues that are unique to their gender. First, I want you to take heart in knowing that being a high achiever is a great thing to be. Throughout history, high achievers have helped to improve our lives and move us forward. Think Ruth Bader Ginsburg and Oprah Winfrey. High achievers get shit done!

I, too, have experienced what so many of my high-achiever clients have experienced—the anxiety that comes from the belief we are not quite good enough, and that we can do better. I'm well acquainted with the crippling self-doubt; the racing mind that never stops and wakes you up in the middle of the night; the taking on of too much; the feeling that there is no time to waste; the depression that comes from total fatigue, stress, and burnout; the competition with others (or yourself); the lack of self-care; and, of course, the monkey on the back of so many high-achieving women— impostor syndrome.

Impostor syndrome is a special pain in the ass because we all have a natural drive to be seen and known for who we truly are. We'll address this issue as well as how you can adapt and connect at work and still be true to your nature. **Rather than fight against your desire to soar high, it's time to acknowledge what's holding you back, harness your drive, and find the happiness so many high achievers find elusive, at work and at home.**

Coaching high achievers has changed my life. It's challenged me to be *my* most authentic self as well. I have never asked my clients to try a strategy I wouldn't commit to myself. And they worked on me! I know the strategies I'm going to share with you work if you adopt them. But I will warn you that change is never easy, and as you grow and develop into the woman you want to be, you will encounter some resistance. As I say to my clients, you may feel anxious as you change behaviors. I'd recommend working on one area of change at a time. And as long as it's manageable, you can be successful, over and over again.

But please be advised that I am not a medical professional. I am not qualified to treat or advise on mental illness, anxiety, or depression. If you ever begin to feel like your emotions are becoming more than you can handle on your own, please seek help from a doctor, therapist, or the emergency room.

If your anxiety or depression is manageable, embrace it as part of your recovery. That's what this book is about—recovering the part of you that has been diminished by your high-achieving self. I promise you that the payoff will be worth it.

The strategies I'll share have come from my experience as a high achiever, and from trial and error with my clients to discover what was most effective. I've incorporated the latest brain research on neuroplasticity, cognitive behavior therapy, Mindfulness, and Transcendental Meditation. I've also included the insights from my own survey to determine high achievers' greatest concerns.

So, let's get started on your journey toward more joy, balance, and even health. You *can* be successful without sacrificing your serenity.

CHAPTER 1:
THE HIGH-ACHIEVER CYCLE

I never dreamed about success. I worked for it.
–Estée Lauder

Throughout the past two decades, I've worked with high-achieving women from around the globe, and within these pages, I'll be sharing my experience with you. Here's the story of one woman I worked with and her journey.

I first met Marie when she was just twenty-six years old and a rising star in an investment firm. Marie had it all going on. She was super smart, laser focused, and highly valued in her organization. Marie's boss knew she was developing a great reputation in the industry and was fearful she would leave if he didn't give her the promotion she was asking for. She was too young to move up, so her boss hired me to help develop her and, truth be known, to slow her ambition so she would stay put.

I learned early in our coaching relationship that nobody would be slowing her down, including me. She had big plans, and the best way I could support her was to help her achieve them.

Over the years, she married a wonderful man, Robert, had two beautiful and healthy children, bought a stunning home in the best neighborhood, and, of course, was highly successful in her career. She continued to break records for being the youngest person promoted at each level in the organization.

Marie enjoyed all the trappings of success: exotic vacations, weekend jaunts to cool cities, a membership at an exclusive country club, expensive clothes, and designer handbags. From the outside looking in, Marie had the perfect life. Only, Marie was miserable.

Marie worked seven days a week. She rarely made it home in time for dinner or to any of her kids' school functions, and she and Robert hadn't had a date night in . . . she couldn't even remember the last time. She justified her behavior by saying as soon as she got to the next level, she could cut back. But the next level would come and go, and Marie couldn't imagine a day in the near future when she could slow down.

The reason Marie couldn't cut back wasn't because she didn't want to, even though she feared the kids were too attached to the nanny, she missed her husband, and she had no social life to speak of. She'd never even been inside the country club after their initial tour. Her ambivalent feelings about cutting back only made her feel guilty.

Marie couldn't cut back because she was surrounded by people who wanted to usurp her as one of the firm's top-performing partners. She had her sights set on senior partner and she couldn't take her foot off the gas until she got there.

There were physical manifestations of Marie's lifestyle as well. She couldn't sleep without the help of a prescription sleep-aid. When she woke up, she felt groggy and irritable. She did keep up with her workouts, but she ate so poorly throughout the day that her body still felt bloated and unbalanced.

There were problems between Robert and Marie too. Robert complained that Marie was distant, always on her phone, and never kept her commitments to her family. Marie's friends felt disconnected as well. They had recently celebrated one of their birthdays, and she hadn't even been invited. Additionally, Marie had stopped attending weekly church services years ago, and she missed the stability her faith had provided her growing up.

But still, Marie did not see a way she could exit her current path without admitting defeat. That's because Marie believed what most high achievers believe: *The more I perform, the more I will accomplish. The more I accomplish, the happier I will be.*

ACHIEVEMENT CYCLE

Do you recognize any of your story in Marie's? You can see the ramifications of your intense drive and ambition around you, but you simply cannot help yourself. You may even rationalize your choices by saying, *Well, someone has to pay the bills,* or *It'll be worth it—they'll see!*

Unfortunately, what most high achievers don't realize is that once you are caught up in the achievement cycle, no amount of achievement will ever make you feel fulfilled. You will never feel like you can let up. The sense of "Okay, I've made it" never comes. It's all temporary.

Maybe that's why you've picked up this book. Maybe you're exhausted by the rat race. Maybe you are sick of yourself. And if someone *gifted* you this book . . . well, maybe they're trying to tell you something!

The truth is, contentment is a struggle for most people. But for a high achiever, contentment can become a myth we chase our entire lives. And before we know it, our friends and family have moved on without us, we're unhappy, disconnected, physically worn down, and all we have to show for it is a list of promotions and a bank account—and *that's* if we're lucky. But what experience, research, and common sense have taught us is that there is so much more to life than professional achievement. In fact, it's arguable that professional achievement should rank fairly low on the list of priorities when compared to family, friends, faith, and mental wellness.

First, you should know you're not alone. Second, you should also know there isn't something "wrong" with you. This book is about growing in self-awareness. It's about understanding ourselves (and the science behind our wiring) better and learning how to live and work a better way.

And don't worry, I'm not going to ask you to sacrifice success or achievement along the way.

POSITIVES AND NEGATIVES OF BEING A HIGH ACHIEVER

The following is a list of actions or thoughts many high achievers admit to having. Let's see if any of these tendencies sound familiar to you:

- You may have anxiety and would like to have more peace.
- You may have a feeling of insecurity.
- You may feel inadequate.
- You are a perfectionist.
- You believe your value is based on what you accomplish.
- You have a fear of failing that impacts your life negatively.
- You may feel like a fraud (impostor).
- You may have depression and would like to feel happier.
- You may lack self-care.

- It's hard for you to be still.
- You're highly logical.
- You often feel impatient.
- You need to feel purposeful or have a goal.
- You believe you could do better.
- You have negative self-talk that diminishes your self-confidence.
- You don't feel productive at the end of the day unless you've checked off every item on your extensive to-do list.
- You sometimes overcommit and overextend yourself.
- You multitask all day, every day.
- You're competitive—with yourself or others.
- You may be proud of your high-achiever handle.
- You would like to feel more satisfied.
- You don't want to waste any time.
- You have a persistent drive to be better and do better.
- You rarely feel satisfied and constantly strive for more.
- You have a desire to prove yourself—especially to anyone who has suggested you aren't capable.
- You feel the need to be recognized for your contribution but often feel ignored.
- You want to have it all.

That list may read a little heavy. Before you start berating yourself (as we high achievers love to do), you should also know that being a high achiever has its advantages, particularly for women navigating the professional world. Besides, we wouldn't exhibit these traits if they didn't—at least to some degree—benefit us in some way.

BENEFITS OF BEING A HIGH ACHIEVER

Achievement brings a lot of advantages. See if any of these resonate with you:

- You've achieved success in your career, often in the early stages.
- Your focus and drive are celebrated.
- You don't let setbacks derail you; you learn from them.
- You're able to inspire others and often become a leader.
- You rely on self-motivation to get things done and meet deadlines.
- You're highly logical and excellent at solving problems.
- You tend to be highly resilient.
- You're creative and innovative.
- You thrive on learning and expanding your skill set.
- You get a lot done.

Being a high achiever doesn't mean you have to sacrifice your serenity. That idea may seem like a lofty or even impossible goal right now, but bear with me. It is possible to be a peaceful high achiever! In fact, many high achievers I've coached are surrounded by friends and family who they schedule time to see often. But the relationships they share aren't often life-giving because a high achiever is constantly feeling as though they're letting others down. We're going to work together to change that in your life.

Being a high achiever is a double-edged sword—there are both favorable and unfavorable consequences. In fact, throughout this book, we'll look at both sides of the sword for the many topics we'll cover pertaining to high achievement.

Yes, being a high achiever can lead to a low-quality of life, but it can also lead to innovation, success, and personal satisfaction. You can be successful and be happy—if you do the work.

HOW DID YOU GET HERE?

Think about it . . . What factors in your life might have resulted in you being a high achiever?

I'm not sure if I was born a high achiever or if it developed over time. But for many of us, there are mitigating factors that combine to develop the latent high achiever in us. The term *nature vs. nurture* was popularized by psychologist Francis Galton in 1884[1], although the concept was debated thousands of years ago by both Plato and Aristotle. The idea is that some of us are born with inherent characteristics and traits while others have those characteristics and traits developed over time by catalytic events.

Which matters more? Nature or nurture? Which has the larger, more impactful effect on a person's life? In recent years, researchers of biopsychology—the study of the brain and behavior—have conducted a number of studies exploring how neurotransmitters influence behavior. We'll talk in greater detail in another chapter about how the brain influences our behavior—it's fascinating!

If you know your family history, think about your genetic inheritance. Though it may not have translated into a role in corporate North America, was your stay-at-home mom a high achiever? Did she cook, clean, run carpool, invent new recipes, take meals to the sick, organize social gatherings, and make sure you were at every practice and club meeting on the calendar? Or maybe it was your grandfather. You often don't have to look far up the family tree to see the characteristics you can see in yourself. My dad would tell me I was working too hard, and I would remind him that the fruit doesn't fall far from the tree.

What are the genetic influences at play when it comes to you being a high achiever?

In social psychology and behaviorism, on the other hand, researchers take into consideration how external factors may influence our behaviors. As you know, our behaviors become patterns, and our patterns become our lifestyles.

Those who argue that nurture plays a more influential role in our behaviors take into account factors such as peer pressure, family structure, childhood experiences, how we were raised, the culture surrounding us, social media influences, and other demographic information that may influence a person's development over time.[2]

Consider your own behaviors. If you had been born to another family, do you think you'd still be a high achiever? Had it not been for your parents' divorce? Had it not been for the school you attended? Had it not been for that one teacher or coach?

What social factors might have contributed to you becoming a high achiever?

EARLY PROGRAMMING

As for you, your upbringing was likely filled with parents, coaches, teachers, friends, and leaders who did their best to provide you with a healthy view of work and a healthy view of self. I'm confident no one said, "I hope Marie grows up to be a miserable high achiever." It's important when we're evaluating our past not to point fingers and place blame.

Recently, a client was sharing an experience she had visiting her daughter's grade 5 classroom. We'll call her Hayley. Hayley is a writer and editor, and she was invited to speak about her career to a room of about fifty students. She'd brought along some of the books she'd published, hoping to inspire young minds to think creatively and dream big for their futures.

Instead, during the middle of her presentation on hard work and success, one of the kids shouted out, "How much money do you make for a book?"

Smiling, Hayley continued her speech.

"Yeah," another kid piped up. "Are you rich?"

Then the entire classroom was off to the races. "I bet you make like a thousand dollars for a book! I bet you're rich!"

"Yeah. What kind of car do you drive? How big is your house?"

Hayley raised a hand to indicate the class should quiet down. She had to address the enormous elephant in the room if she wanted to finish up. "I make a different amount of money for every book I write," she said. "I make just enough."

Thankfully, Mr. Joyner jumped in the conversation and bailed Hayley out—finally. She later told me she was surprised by how long it took the teacher to intervene. My guess is that he was curious how much Hayley earned as well!

Hayley's experience is an important illustration. From a very early age, we define success one way: wealth. In fact, a 2016 study by psychologists out of the University of Wisconsin-Madison and Yale was conducted to investigate how children respond to wealth cues.[3]

The goal of the study was to investigate whether children used cues most commonly associated with wealth differences in society to guide their evaluation of others. The study revealed that four- to five-year-olds expressed preferences for children who were paired with high-wealth cues. Children ages four to six used wealth cues to infer people's social standings (whether or not the people were well-liked or popular), and children ages five to nine used wealth cues to guide their evaluations of and their actions toward other people.

Kids sense that wealth has power. They ask questions related to wealth: "Are we rich? Are we poor? Why does so-and-so have a bigger house than us? Why does so-and-so drive that kind of car?" Children are socialized into believing that wealthier people have better, more satisfying lives. In this experience, many of us grow up believing we have to "have more" to "be more," and likewise, "do more" to get there.

Is it any wonder that kids become programmed from such an early age to believe the only way a person can be happy is for them to have a lot of money?

AVERAGE HIGH ACHIEVER UPBRINGING

Let's say the typical high achiever's name is Olivia. It's likely Olivia showed academic promise from an early age. Maybe Olivia's earliest memories are of her being affirmed for her aptitude and accomplishments in the classroom. She was confident in elementary school and even tested to enter the gifted program. Once placed in enrichment classes, Olivia's drive to succeed was ratcheted up. She didn't have the cognitive ability to name her compulsion just yet, but internally, she wanted to prove she was worthy of her new challenge.

Middle school brought new challenges, but Olivia met them with gusto. She preened under the attention she received from being in the "special" classes and thoroughly enjoyed the way it made her feel to be told she was "gifted." By high school, Olivia found herself surrounded by other students who thought and performed like she did. She played on the school's lacrosse team where she, to no one's surprise, excelled. She joined a myriad of clubs and was on the debate team.

College followed much of the same pattern. Olivia out studied, outperformed, and out clubbed all the girls in her sorority, graduating in the top 10 percent of her class. She was offered a full-time position at the company she'd interned at and set her sights on accomplishing her next goal: Team Lead.

Your story may not mirror Olivia's exactly. Maybe you experienced a catalytic event like a divorce at home that propelled you into your studies. Maybe you grew up in poverty and knew that achieving academically was your only way out. Or maybe, like Olivia, you never experienced much affirmation outside of achievement-related affirmation, and the feeling it gave you became your addiction.

Like most addictions, your achievement addiction crept up on you without your even knowing it. Maybe you haven't realized until right this moment that *that* is the high you are constantly chasing.

Well, consider this book your entry into achievement rehab. And just like working a program, we're going to walk step-by-step through your recovery!

MY STORY: A HIGH ACHIEVER IS MADE

I didn't have a typical childhood—especially for a high achiever. I was often sick and had several procedures during my formative years that caused me to miss a *ton* of school. A good friend of mine would bring my schoolwork home for me, which I completed easily on my own. And though I never failed any subjects, I also never gained enough momentum to dig in or feel good at anything academically. I was extroverted, but I never saw myself as smart or a good student.

While my high-achiever tendencies didn't get the chance to shine through my academics, I always had a thirst for a paycheck. I loved earning money, and I was good at it too. When I was thirteen, one of my friends mentioned she'd been asked to babysit but wasn't interested in the job.

"Give them my name!" I told her. I couldn't imagine not wanting to work.

From there, I had a thriving babysitting business that was in very high demand. I'm serious! Families liked me because, despite my age, I was responsible, prompt, and dependable. By the time I was fifteen, I was ready to work outside of homes. I got my first retail job, immediately followed by a second at a large department store. I enjoyed the feeling of accomplishment I felt with each interaction, each completed sale, and especially with each paycheck.

The summer between grade 11 and grade 12, I got my dream job at an animal clinic. At the time, I imagined I'd grow up to be a veterinarian. I even changed high schools in order to take this job. Every day as soon as school let out, I'd make the twenty-minute walk to the clinic and worked until 6 p.m. I'd go home, have dinner, do schoolwork, and go to bed to wake up and do it again—on Saturdays too. And I loved it. Of course, it helped that my boyfriend worked with me at the clinic.

The week after I graduated from high school, I visited a friend's beach cottage where we all discussed what we were going to do next. In Ontario, Canada, at the time, you could attend grade 13 before leaving for university. Or you could go to college after your senior year. I didn't want to do either.

My friend pointed out an ad for a hospital. They were offering a yearlong training program for cardiology techs. I called them that same day, and they informed me they were conducting interviews that afternoon and called me in. I ran home, changed into the one dress I owned, and headed to the hospital. The man who interviewed me never asked my age or about my level of education. I'm sure he thought I was older than eighteen, and I was elated when I learned I had gotten the position. My brother knew an executive at the hospital and mentioned I was applying. I found out they had many applicants, and my brother's contact ensured that I was considered.

That being said, I had no idea how intense the job would be! They trained us on site for a few weeks, then sent us to a nearby college for an intensive class. After that, I was a certified cardiology tech running heart tests on critical patients. If I told you some of the things I witnessed and the traumatic situations I was a part of during my work at the hospital, you'd be shocked. Especially during the overnight shift.

It was during this job that I realized I had grit. We'll talk more about grit later, but I've yet to meet a high achiever who doesn't demonstrate it. There was something inside that pushed me, propelled me forward, to work harder and want more. I dreamed of doing more—and more and more.

One thing I'd like all of us high achievers to recognize is that a large amount of our ambition is attached to a feeling. The way it *feels* to make money. The way it *feels* to get a promotion. The way it *feels* to be affirmed or complimented.

I like to think we're a result of a combination of our natural wiring, early programming, and our environments.

Regardless of how we got here, I want you to know that this book is not intended to change who you are. Instead, its intent is to help you leverage all the positives of being a high achiever and to help you manage all the negatives therein as well.

As we work together to find solutions for a better way of living, I want us to first start by embracing one simple fact: **We don't have to apologize for who we are.**

Remember Marie from earlier in this chapter? Well, Marie and I are still very much in touch. To no one's surprise, she is still extremely successful. In fact, she's continued to rise in the ranks professionally and has checked off quite a few boxes on her goals and dreams lists. When I last spoke to Marie she said, "I couldn't be happier. But it's still hard work."

Marie has conquered her stress and self-doubt. She's successful, and she's also serene. But this isn't something that just "happened" for Marie. She's worked very hard at it—and she continues to do the work.

It wasn't that her boss hired me that helped Marie. It was her willingness to listen and try new things. It was her openness to feedback and a different perspective. It was the countless hours of inner work. And much of that work produces delayed, intangible results—a high achiever's least favorite type of result! But over time the compounding effect is lifelong change that will transform your quality of life, not to mention the lives of those around you.

Ultimately, Marie had the problem all of us do. She believed she'd be happier if she accomplished more in work. She had set her expectations so high that even if she worked every minute of every day, she still wouldn't have been satisfied had she not gotten help. But like I said, hiring a coach or even reading this book won't help you. I'll repeat it: You have to do the work.

Some good news? Work is our specialty.

LET'S GET PRACTICAL

In this section, we'll take what we've read and apply it to our lives. Words and theories remain words and theories unless we put them into practice.

HIGH ACHIEVER QUIZ

Let's gauge your high-achiever level. For all the statements below, mark "Me" or "Not Me" accordingly.

	ME	NOT ME
I'm rarely satisfied with my accomplishments.		
I frequently work past regular work hours or take work home.		
Work commitments usually trump my personal life.		
I have difficulty delegating tasks because I can do them better.		
Once I achieve one goal, I immediately set my sights on the next one.		
I find it hard to relax and often feel guilty for not working.		
I hold myself to a much higher standard than I hold others.		
I feel like if I allow myself to coast or "take my foot off the gas," I will fall behind.		
In a choice between me time and work time, I usually choose work.		
If it weren't for my work, I wouldn't know who I am or what to do with myself.		
I constantly compare myself to others and worry I don't measure up to their success.		
I'm a perfectionist and am rarely satisfied.		
I feel constant pressure to prove myself.		
I am highly competitive. If I'm not the best, I will work at it until I am.		
When I'm engrossed in work, I often skip meals or personal responsibilities.		
The people who love me most complain that I work too much.		

SCORING: Count your "Me" responses.

0–5: Minor High Achiever

Your nature as a high achiever is not dominant in your life. You likely have a balanced approach to setting goals and managing expectations. While you may have moments of drive and ambition, you know how to prioritize and avoid overwhelming yourself with excessive pressure. You have a healthy work–life balance and understand the importance of self-care. You will still want to read this book to learn how to increase your self-care.

6–10: Moderate High Achiever

You are a moderate high achiever who strives for a more balanced approach managing work and your personal life. Your ambition drives you to set and achieve goals, but you are also cognizant of the risk for burnout if you don't make time for yourself and those who matter to you. You're reading this book to learn how to achieve that elusive balance you know will ultimately bring you happiness.

11–16: Strong High Achiever

Your nature as a high achiever is very dominant in your life. Your strong desire to constantly achieve bigger and better goals for yourself has likely resulted in a significant feeling of being off-balance in any area that isn't work related. Others may even call you an overachiever. While you relish chasing and surpassing your goals, you need to be mindful of the pitfalls of solely focusing so much of your time and attention on the future. It's time to celebrate your wins today. Consider reaching out to friends, family, or professionals for support in dealing with the stress your insatiable desire for success brings into your life.

Knowing where you stand is critical to knowing where you want to go. Our goal through this book will be to lower that score as much as possible, bringing you balance and serenity.

THE WHEEL OF LIFE: GAINING PERSPECTIVE ON YOUR UNIQUE JOURNEY

In the whirlwind of achievements, ambitions, and aspirations, high-achieving women often tread a path that is brilliantly illuminated in certain areas, while others remain shadowed. The notion of a balanced life is elusive and, perhaps, even a myth. However, the power lies not in achieving a perfect balance but in understanding the harmony and dissonance of our lives, and making conscious choices based on that understanding.

Enter "The Wheel of Life." This tool doesn't promise balance; instead, it offers clarity. It provides a panoramic view, allowing you to gauge the various facets of your life. By assessing these facets, you not only discern where you might want to channel more energy and focus but also identify areas that, when nurtured, can ripple positive effects into other domains of your life.

For many high achievers, the spotlight often shines brightest on career milestones and tangible accomplishments. It's not uncommon to prioritize one segment, sometimes at the unintended expense of others. But here's the thing: The Wheel of Life isn't a tool of judgment or an instrument to instill guilt. Instead, it's an opportunity—a chance to take stock, to introspect, and, most importantly, to make empowered decisions. By rating various aspects of your life, you embark on a self-awareness journey, gleaning insights that can guide you toward a life more closely aligned with your heart's desires.

Embrace this tool, not as a critique, but as a compass. Let it illuminate the path you're on and help you navigate toward a life of fulfillment, however you define it.

Review the eight areas on the Wheel of Life. The wheel must, when put together, create a view of a balanced life for you. If necessary, you can split categories to add in something that is missing for you.

The eight sections in the Wheel of Life represent balance. This exercise will help clarify priorities for goal setting, allowing you to plan so your life is closer to their definition of balance. A few notes on balance:

- The meaning of balance is uniquely personal. Avoid comparing yourself to others because what they consider balance could be off-putting to you.
- Balance must be assessed over time. So, a regular check on how balanced you are can highlight useful

patterns and help you learn even more about yourself. I suggest redoing this exercise every few months so you can take stock and adjust your goals as needed.

- Acknowledge that the scales of life are rarely perfectly balanced. The goal is to keep them relatively stable (think 55/45 rather than 80/20).

Think about the various areas of your life and rank your level of satisfaction with each one. Place a value between 1 (very dissatisfied) and 10 (fully satisfied) against each area to show how satisfied you are currently with these elements in your life.

- Career: Your general job satisfaction
- Health: Your emotional and physical well-being
- Home: Your overall satisfaction with your physical surroundings
- Family/Friends: Your relationships
- Money: Your overall financial security
- Personal Growth: Expanding your knowledge, spiri-tuality, or sense of service
- Recreation: What you do for fun or relaxation
- Romantic Relationship: Your relationship with your partner/spouse

After you've ranked them, think about what success feels like for each area. Write a short description of "success" for each section of your Wheel of Life:

Success in Section 1:

Success in Section 2:

Success in Section 3:

Success in Section 4:

Success in Section 5:

Success in Section 6: ....
....
....
....

Success in Section 7: ....
....
....
....

Success in Section 8: ....
....
....
....

Now, rank your level of satisfaction with each area of your life by drawing a line across each segment. Here's an example:

The new perimeter of the circle represents your "Wheel of Life."

THE WHEEL OF LIFE

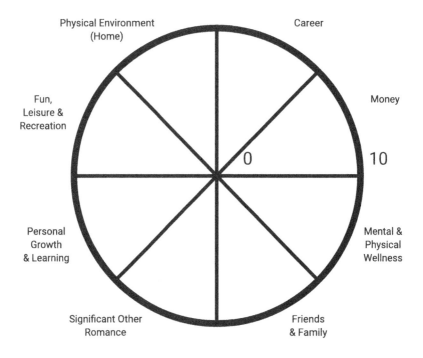

REFLECTION

Looking at the wheel, here are some questions to take you deeper:

- Are there any surprises for you?
- How do you feel about your life as you look at your wheel?
- How do you currently spend time in these areas?

- How would you like to spend time in these areas?

- Which of these elements would you most like to improve?

- How could you make space for these changes?

- Can you make the necessary changes on your own?

- What help and cooperation from others might you need?

- What would make that a score of 10?

- What would a score of 10 look like?

CHAPTER 2:
TAMING THE STRESS BEAST
AND AVOIDING BURNOUT

Stress is a ridiculous thing that society has made up
so that we feel like we're doing something.
–Arianna Huffington,
cofounder of *The Huffington Post*

"I am *so* stressed out."

How often in a week do you think those words? How often in a *day,* even? If you're a high achiever, it's probably a lot—even if it's not something you verbalize. I mean, how could we? If we admitted we were having difficulty managing our tasks and responsibilities, it would be like admitting failure, right? The truth is, many of us could have master's degrees in impression management.

Someone approaches us out of concern: "How are you? You seem stressed."

"Who, me?" we respond, juggling a laptop, phone, ear buds, and notes from a meeting we just left. "No, I'm not stressed. Just have a lot going on!"

Because we're self-protective, and because we don't want to let anyone down, we may not even admit to ourselves that we're completely overwhelmed and one email request, Slack message, or Asana ping away from burnout. No one puts on a more convincing performance than a high achiever. After all, we've built our entire persona around the idea that we *can* do it all. If we can't, in fact, do it all, that would be a blow to not only our ego but also to our identity.

If we were honest, we'd say we are stressed. We're driven. We're hungry. We don't want to do well, we want to *crush* it. And most of the time, we can. But because we aren't often realistic about what we can reasonably accomplish in a set amount of time, we overcommit. And because our ambition can outweigh our common sense, we work ourselves ragged to do the undoable. That's who we are—we get shit done.

Or perhaps you don't think you're stressed. But maybe your thoughts sound more like:

"I'll never get all of this done on time."
→ The pressure of looming deadlines makes tasks feel insurmountable.

"I can't make a mistake; it would ruin everything."
→ The fear of failure comes from believing one's success is precarious.

"Why does everything always go wrong for me?"
→ A sense of hopelessness or a pattern of negative thinking seems personal or never ending.

"I don't have control over anything in my life."
> → Having too much on the go leads to feeling stressed and overwhelmed.

"I'm letting everyone down."
> → An overwhelmed person might feel like they're not doing anything right.

"I can't handle this."
> → A stressed person may begin to feel helpless and lose confidence.

"What if something bad happens?"

> → Anxiety about the future and the unknown can lead to catastrophic thinking, where the mind jumps to the worst possible outcomes.

"I should be doing better than this."
> → Playing the comparison game rarely makes one feel good about themselves.

"I don't have time for myself anymore."
> → A stressed person often ignores their own well-being to focus on other tasks they perceive as more important.

"No one understands what I'm going through."
> → A sense of isolation or belief that others can't comprehend the stress may further intensify the feelings of anxiety.

Avoiding the term "stress" does not make you less stressed. If any of the above thoughts sound familiar to you, you are categorically stressed out.

CHASING THE RUSH: MY LOVE AFFAIR WITH STRESS

I know a thing or two (or 2,000!) about stress. In the past, I was the embodiment of every bustling city's ethos: fast-paced, goal-oriented, and ceaselessly striving for the next big thing. As the owner of an executive search firm, I found that my days revolved around juggling responsibilities and chasing deadlines. To many, I might have looked like a scene straight out of a movie—I was always on the move, coffee in one hand and my phone in the other, darting from one meeting to the next.

There's something incredibly intoxicating about the constant buzz of stress. It's a secret most high achievers harbor, and I'll admit, I was addicted. You might wonder why anyone would voluntarily engage in such a whirlwind lifestyle. Well, stress, I realized, was like a drug that released potent brain chemicals. The adrenaline, the cortisol, and the dopamine made me feel alive, invincible even. That rush of knowing that I was indispensable, that my clients depended on me, and that I was always on top of things gave me a sense of purpose and significance.

Onlookers might see it as commitment, but there's a dark side to this relentless drive. Every morning I'd be up at the crack of dawn, my sneakers hitting the pavement before the world even stirred. I promised myself evenings of leisurely reading, but often they'd culminate in a glass or two of wine—my brain's desperate plea for relaxation.

Every week I'd have this ritual. On Fridays, I'd step into the serene ambiance of the massage clinic right next to my office building at 4 p.m. sharp. It was my little escape, my self-reward for yet another week of hard work. But it was on that massage table, with gentle hands working through the tensed fabric of my muscles, that I'd feel the full weight of my stress. I'd wince in pain, feeling every golf ball-sized knot in my shoulder, every tight strand in my neck. But just like every other addict, I'd brush it off and promise myself, "Just one more week of this and then I'll slow down."

Admitting that you're addicted to stress is hard, especially when the world around you often equates busyness with importance. We're made to believe that unless we're running on fumes, we're not doing enough. That unless our calendars are chock-a-block with meetings, we're not valuable. But what we often forget in this relentless chase is the toll it takes on our bodies and minds.

We spend our whole lives chasing dreams yet fail to recognize the simplest of truths: our bodies aren't indestructible. Those weekly massages were more than just relaxation sessions, they were my body's SOS signals. But it took me years to understand that I had a choice.

Stress can be addictive, but like any addiction, it comes at a price. Today I share my story, not as a cautionary tale, but as a friendly reminder: to remind you to listen to your body, to understand that ambition need not come at the cost of health, and, most importantly, to recognize the signs before stress becomes your drug of choice.

WHAT IS STRESS, ANYWAY?

When you view the potentially powerful and harmful effects of stress—not just to your mental health but to your physical health as well—is it any wonder there are hundreds of thousands of articles, books, podcasts, and products produced every year to help us manage our stress? But what if I were to tell you we've gotten it wrong? Or partly wrong?

Let me explain.

Hungarian endocrinologist and father of stress research Dr. Hans Selye profoundly stated: "It's not stress that kills us, it's our reaction to stress."[4] Stress isn't all bad. It's highly motivating. It's proof we care. And it can maximize our performance—*if* it's managed well. And that's a big if. Before writing this book, I conducted a battery of surveys given to women who identified as high achievers. The resounding response was that the majority not only identified as being under daily stress, they also admitted to having poor stress-management skills.

But if we can leverage our stress, if we can put a few stress-management tools in our toolbox, we can experience the "good" stress. We can also operate at a higher capacity. See, we often confuse the feelings of stress with productivity, but that's not always the case. We all know stress is a part of everyday life and a normal response to day-to-day pressures. We may even joke about the amount of stress we're under without realizing the far-reaching effects it has on our overall well-being. According to The American Psychological Society: "Stress involves changes affecting nearly every system of the body, influencing how people feel and behave. By causing mind–body changes, stress contributes directly to psychological and physiological disorder and disease and affects mental and physical health, reducing quality of life."[5]

Let's explore the effects of stress on your physical and psychological health.

Psychologically: From a mental health perspective, stress creates an imbalance in the brain that triggers feelings of overwhelm. Over time, these feelings can lead to anxiety, depression, aggression, or burnout.

Physiologically: From a biological standpoint, stress activates the body's fight-or-flight response. When faced with a stressor, the brain signals the adrenal glands to release hormones like adrenaline and cortisol. These hormones prepare the body to respond to the threat by increasing heart rate, blood pressure, and energy supplies. Prolonged exposure to stress can lead to chronic health issues, such as heart disease and weakened immune function. (More on this later.)

Stress is an uncomfortable feeling that can lead to worry. But is stress the same thing as worry? At its core, worry is simply an attempt to avoid unpleasant consequences by adopting repetitive thought patterns. For example, we love to wrestle with a wide variety of "what if" questions:

- What if people realize I don't know what I'm doing?
- What if I'm not really cut out for this job?
- What if I work too much and lose my friends and family?
- What if I'm never promoted?
- What if I'm never respected as much as my peers?
- What if I fail?

We don't particularly enjoy asking ourselves these questions, but sometimes we can't help it. It might feel like worrying or brooding over our problems is productive, but worry is not the same as "thinking through" our problems. Worry is also not the same thing as confronting a situation and trying to address it. **By obsessing over our problems, we gain a false sense of control. And we high achievers like our control.**

Conversely, where worry is a mental habit, fear is an instinctive reaction—usually in the face of a perceived threat. Fear is a survival trait that has been honed through the human evolutionary process. Once upon a time, humans lived in far more barbaric conditions. And a perceived threat was often an actual threat. Think: On your hunt for tonight's dinner, you encounter a tiger in the jungle you inhabit. Talk about fear! But because our brains are responsible for these reactions, we can often feel our fear and stress spiraling out of control.

Our reactions to fear are actually quite fascinating, and they're all rooted inside the intricate and sometimes mysterious caverns of our brains. I promise, we're going to get back to stress, but first, let's study the science behind it.

Your brain is made up of many different parts, but for our purpose, we're going to focus on the limbic system. The limbic system is a collection of structures involved in processing emotion and memory, including the hippocampus, the amygdala, and the hypothalamus. The amygdala, a small, almond-shaped structure, is responsible for the fight-or-flight response.

The amygdala is *also* considered the emotional center of the brain, which if you think about it, is problematic—because we know that negative thoughts can trigger the amygdala. Rick Hanson PhD, founder of the Wellspring Institute for Neuroscience and Contemplative Wisdom, also calls the amygdala "the alarm bell of your brain."[6] So if your alarm bell lives in the same house as your emotions, you're bound to have some tricky emotional responses that may or may not reflect reality.

I was home alone the other night while my husband was out. I'm not a person who is easily frightened—I've spent my fair share of time on the road too! But I was up late working, and I kept hearing this scratching noise on my front door. The more I listened, the more I was *convinced* someone was seconds away from using a jimmy to pop the lock open on the door.

Then my dog started going bonkers. He ran toward the sound, barking his little head off. Finally, to prove *both* of us wrong, I got up from the sofa and marched to the front door. The closer I got to the door, the louder and more distinct the sound was. Now, in my mind, I *knew* there was a logical explanation for what I was hearing. I mean, either it was the world's slowest break-in or something innocuous was creating the sound. But as I edged near, my heart rate increased, my breathing became a little heavy, and I felt a growing sense of panic rising out of my belly and into my throat.

In a dramatic flurry I'm thankful no one was present to witness, I wrenched open the door. And there was my culprit—right before my very eyes. The biggest, baddest, most alarming pamphlet you've ever seen.

That's right. It was one of those flyers companies tape to your door to solicit your business. It was still wafting in the breeze. I imagine it had been brushing against the door frame creating the dreaded scratching sound I'd gotten momentarily mortally terrified over.

All those responses—the heart rate, the breathing—those were a result of my body's fight-or-flight response. My adrenaline was pumping, preparing me for whatever I'd find on the other side of the door—which I was convinced was an axe murderer there to kill me.

But once that fight-or-flight instinct kicks in, powerful chemicals flood our brains—chemicals like adrenaline and cortisol. Adrenaline, as you probably know, increases your heart rate. It makes your blood pump more rapidly and your breath come faster. It also gives you an energy boost. But unless you're about to run a sprint race, too much energy can feel like . . . too much. Along with a myriad of other effects, one of the things cortisol does is suppress our immune system, giving us that "my stomach just dropped to the floor" sensation.

Our bodies are now in an all-out war against whatever our perceived threat may be. While our brains may see the pamphlet and understand it's perfectly harmless, the chemicals coursing through our bodies are screaming just the opposite.

In time, yes, our hormone levels will return to normal. However, when we're constantly experiencing stressful situations, our alarm bells ring all day long. This long-term activation of our stress response and the ever-presence of adrenaline and cortisol in our systems can have harmful effects on our bodies, like:

- Anxiety
- Depression
- Digestive problems
- Headaches
- Muscle tension and pain
- Heart disease, heart attack, high blood pressure, and stroke
- Sleep problems
- Weight gain
- Memory and concentration impairment

Long-term stress can wreak havoc on our mental and physical health. Therefore, it's important for our own well-being to be able to limit and manage stress to the short term in our day-to-day lives.

SHORT-TERM STRESS VS. LONG-TERM STRESS

Short-term, or acute, stress occurs in response to immediate threats. This type of stress can be beneficial in certain situations. For instance, the stress you feel when you have a deadline approaching can help you focus better and work more efficiently. It can temporarily boost the immune system and provide the body with a surge of energy. Also, short-term stress can be exciting and invigorating, like the feeling you get on a roller coaster or when you're about to perform on stage. The key here is that the body has time to recover and reset after each stressful episode.

Long-term, or chronic, stress poses more problems when it's consistent and there is no opportunity for the body to recover. Examples of long-term stress can be dealing with a high-pressure job, financial difficulties, chronic illness, or another traumatic challenge.

While short-term stress can sometimes serve as a positive reinforcement, helping us perform better and navigate through intense situations, long-term chronic stress can be detrimental to both our mental and physical health. Keeping stress levels under control and ensuring stress does not become chronic are essential for maintaining a balanced mental and physical state. It's a lesson I learned the hard way.

MY STRESS STORY

I want to share my own experience that led to an understanding of my own stress response and its impact on my body. Several years back I was unfortunately exposed to toxic mold. Although I meditated regularly, managed negative self-talk, and supported myself with self-care, I still got very sick. So sick, in fact, an MRI showed that I had swelling in two parts of my brain.

What seemed like a never-ending array of medical tests confirmed the negative impact of the mold that created mycotoxins in my body. It wasn't lost on my brain that mycotoxins include the word *toxins*. Fear took over, and my life rotated around my diagnosis and the mold. I feared mold and looked for it everywhere I went. *Is that mold?* All day long. Several times a day I took medication that just reminded me of how ill I was.

My doctor recommended a five-day program called Dynamic Neural Retraining System.[7] I was fortunate that it was offered in my city and assumed that I would be a day student. The instructors suggested I take a risk and stay at the hotel, which I was sure had mold. Somehow, I was able to overcome my fear and I did end up getting a room. By that point I was just desperate to feel better physically *and* mentally.

This program was a miracle for me and for many of the other thirty participants. Over the course of five days we learned how the limbic system affects the body. Basically, my limbic system was always on red alert by looking for mold, which triggered my amygdala to produce cortisol and adrenaline. By calming the limbic system, the amygdala could relax. The program taught me how to change the chemistry in my brain from bathing it in cortisol and adrenaline to the feel-good brain chemicals of dopamine, oxytocin, and serotonin.

That program changed my life. I was still full of toxins, but my brain was no longer in overdrive. I started to heal. Understanding that I could control how my brain functioned was, and still is, empowering. I share this understanding with my clients every day.

"GOOD" STRESS?

We've already discussed the idea that stress isn't exclusively a bad thing—because it's not. In fact, as I've already mentioned, a certain amount of stress can be beneficial. Let's take a deeper look at "good" stress.

In 1998, thirty-thousand adults in the United States were asked how much stress they had experienced in the last year. Then they were asked if they believed stress to be harmful to their health. As a follow-up to that study, eight years later in 2006, researchers delved into public records to tabulate how many of those participants were still alive. Here are their results: 43 percent of the participants who had stated they were experiencing high levels of stress were more likely to have passed. But that increased risk was *only* applied to the participants who had also said that stress was harmful to their health.[8] Isn't that wild?

The only conclusion to be made is that how we view stress matters more than the stress itself. Stress alone won't kill you, but fearing your stress might.

A BETTER WAY TO LEVERAGE STRESS

Short-term stress can have positive effects as well. This concept, known as "eustress," refers to a beneficial type of stress that can enhance function. Here are three potentially positive results of acute stress that have been researched:

- Improved cognitive function resulting in sharper focus and decision-making
- Enhanced immune response enabling the body to home in on an injury
- Improved performance by boosting motivation for tackling a task

So, how do we begin to view our stress differently? Especially when our bodies and brains are reacting violently?

First, you must understand that you will never completely be "unstressed." You're not going to wake up one day and say, "Hey, absolutely nothing stresses me out. Life is breezy and easy!" If that *were* to happen, you'd probably get stressed out about not being stressed out. The goal is to help you find the positives in the short-term stress that is unavoidable, which will mitigate prolonged stress. It's about changing your mindset about stress to help you realize you *can* rewrite your brain's ability to "snap out of it" and leverage your stress for good.

Mindfulness and *Transcendental Meditation* are two terms that you're probably aware of that will help with stress relief and relaxation, but you might be unsure of how to incorporate them into your busy schedule.

Mindfulness is the easiest way to introduce meditation into your life—it's simply the act of being in the moment and connected to whatever you're doing. It may sound simple, but it's very difficult for so many of us because our mind is usually running a mile a minute in a zig-zag pattern, jumping from item to item on our seemingly endless to-do list or replaying a past interaction or conversation (with a colleague or family member or even an angry driver in traffic). Or we're on autopilot, totally unaware of our actions. How often do we sit down with a cup of coffee and really experience it? With the Mindfulness practice, we are aware of smelling the coffee's aroma, of feeling the warmth of the mug in our hands, of savoring the first sip, etc. Now multiply this by every single act you do throughout the day—from showering to eating to driving to simply breathing. It's possible and beneficial to take a few moments of mindfulness throughout your day. If it seems difficult, start by focusing on your breaths and thinking about your actions. Even washing your hands can become a small moment to pause, reset, and breathe.

Transcendental Meditation is a specific meditation from ancient India, which was revived by Maharishi Mahesh Yogi in 1955, that involves reaching the fourth level of consciousness (after awake, sleeping, and dreaming) to achieve inner peace and well-being. It is a mantra-based meditation technique that requires one-on-one instruction to learn. So many successful individuals swear by it, from Paul McCartney to Oprah Winfrey. But I speak from experience when I say that it has been a game changer for me. By incorporating both Mindfulness and Transcendental Meditation into my daily life, I am happier, calmer, and more at peace than ever before, which translates into being a more fulfilled and capable person in all aspects of my life.

HOW TO REWIRE YOUR BRAIN

People often refer to an intriguing urban legend about a frog in hot water. If you plunge a frog into boiling water, it'll bolt out immediately. However, say you put that same frog in a pot of lukewarm water and slowly, ever so slowly, turn up the heat, the frog will stay put, oblivious to the rising temperature until it meets an unfortunate, boiling end. This so-called frog in the water phenomenon is due to an inability to recognize and respond to gradual changes in our mental and emotional "temperature."

This allegory is popularly used to illustrate how smoothly instilled changes stand a stronger chance of greater success. It also casts light on a peculiar trait of our own human psychology: we often become oblivious to the steadily creeping influences around us, often allowing them to dictate our lives. We tend to accommodate these constant conditions, adapting and adjusting, almost like the frog in the gradually heating water.

Suddenly, though, we might find ourselves in a "boiling" situation: life spiraling out of control due to cumulative minor factors we failed to acknowledge. It's somewhat the nature of our lives when we let things become excessive and unchecked. Just like the blithely ignorant frog, we might get caught in steadily mounting troubles, and one day we wake up feeling like we're in hot water.

That's why we need to create habits to constantly keep

a pulse on the climate of our stress levels. One of which is retraining our brains through neuroplasticity.

Neuroplasticity is the concept that our brains are malleable. They are capable of being rewired in response to new experiences. Daniela Kaufer and Elizabeth Kirby are stress researchers at the University of California. In 2013, they exposed lab rats to a few hours of moderate stress. Initially, the rats showed little response to the stressors. But two weeks later, after repeated exposure, their brains had developed new neural connections that actually *improved* their performance on memory tests.[9]

The same science applies to us. As long as stress doesn't bring us to the point of serious misery, or trauma, exposure to intermittent bursts of moderate stress helps our nerve cells to increase. Kirby said of her findings: "Intermittent stressful events are probably what keep the brain alert, and you perform better when you are alert."

And the rats have more to teach us! According to a 2012 American study, rats exposed to different types of stress also displayed more infection-fighting white cells in their blood stream.[10] So, while chronic, long-term stress will harm our bodies, a moderate amount of stress may actually protect us from disease.

Now, understand, I'm not saying that all stress is healthy. We already know our limbic system can work against us if we're not careful. However, the point to be learned here is that moderate stress can actually make us perform better and even boost our immune systems. Knowing this helps us contextualize stressful moments, and even stressful days. Positive self-talk might sound like "Hey, that was a tough day. I was really stressed out about that meeting. But the meeting is over, it went well, and now I don't have to feel that stress anymore."

In his book *The MindBody Workbook*, Dr. David Schechter makes the comparison between working out and physically improving our body to changing our negative thoughts to improving our mental health. "Learning to think differently is part of how we learn to get rid of the pain pathways and replace them with new circuitry. Affirmations can help us stop bad habits and pain is a kind of habit that we need to break, in a neurologic sense," he says.[11]

This practice over time can actually rewire your brain to view moderate stress as a good thing. Which will make you feel, well, less stressed!

MIRROR NEURONS

Mirror neurons represent a fascinating and significant discovery. These specialized neurons, found in the brain, are responsible for a remarkable phenomenon: they activate not only when we perform an action but also when we observe someone else performing that action. Essentially, they enable us to "mirror" the experiences of others, contributing to our ability to empathize and understand their actions and emotions. When we consider the impact of our thoughts on our behavior and how others perceive us, the role of mirror neurons becomes even more intriguing.

If we change our internal narrative, this shift is reflected in our external behavior—often subtly, but significantly. For example, changing your internal dialogue from "I'm not confident" to "I'm confident" could alter your posture, you may find yourself making eye contact, your tone of voice could be deeper and louder, and your mannerisms convey confidence to others. The mirror neurons in the brains of those around us respond to these changes, leading them to perceive us as more confident. This is an unconscious, neurological response that shapes their perception of us and, in turn, their reactions and behaviors towards us. By changing our thoughts and the resulting behaviors, we can indirectly influence how others see and respond to us, creating a cycle of positive interaction and perception.

Once we are aware of our thoughts, we can actively work to alter them. Changing our thoughts is not an overnight process but a deliberate practice that requires persistence and patience. The power to choose and change our thoughts is one of the most empowering tools we possess. It allows us to take control of our mental narrative, shape our behavior, and ultimately create the life we desire.

PRACTICAL STEPS TO REWIRE YOUR BRAIN

VISUALIZATIONS

One tool I use for brain rewiring with my clients (and that I use personally) is visualizations. At its core, future visualization is a practice where you mentally envision potential outcomes for your life. These visualizations can range from visualizing a successful business presentation to imagining personal milestones, like achieving an ideal physical health exam or visualizing a positive family outing. Anything that makes you feel happy, calm, or at ease.

The practice may sound silly—especially since there is no "tangible" result, which high achievers love. Sometimes I do my visualizations standing up, but you can sit or lie down. It may be awkward and not always doable, but if you say your visualization out loud, it's easier to stay focused.

It's important to know that it's not important what you visualize. You could visualize something you know will never happen, and your brain will respond the same way—immerse that brain in wonderful chemicals of dopamine, oxytocin, and serotonin. The brain believes what you tell it to believe. Those nasty chemicals of cortisol and adrenaline don't have a chance!

One of my visualizations is that I'm in Banff, Canada:

There is a sloping trail in front of me. The trees are so tall. The sky is so blue. The sun filters through the tree branches and I see patterns of light and shadows on the ground. I feel so grateful to be here and I feel so happy that I'm here in this beautiful place. I feel the crisp, cool air on my face and as I breathe in, it's like I'm breathing in joy. With each breath, I feel my body stronger and stronger.

As I walk, I feel the soft crunch of pine needles and dry leaves and I have this sense that all is right with the world. That everything is unfolding as it should. I feel a sense of peace. It starts in my solar plexus and radiates out. I'm so happy.

I hear the birds and the sound of babbling brook nearby, and I think about how lucky I am. I'm the luckiest person alive. The air has a smell of pine, damp earth, and a hint of wildflowers. I'm where I belong. This is what I'm meant for. A sense of gratitude is almost overwhelming, and I notice that I have tears on my face. Tears of joy.

I've never felt so free. So free, and I have this sense that I can do anything. I'm powerful. I'm strong.

I'm at the top of the trail now. I can see for miles. I feel humbled that I can witness such beauty. I feel so happy. I feel the joy wash over me and I see it as this bright blue smoke that envelopes me. I've never felt such joy. I take several deep breaths and feel joyful, powerful, grateful.

When you visualize something wonderful with all the details to provoke the feelings (it's the feelings that count and not how you get there), your brain is bathed in the wonderful DOSE chemicals—Dopamine, Oxytocin, Serotonin, and Endorphins. A DOSE a day keeps the cortisol at bay!

SHIELDING YOURSELF FOR SERENITY

For as long as I can remember, I've been a bona fide news junkie. Every morning, while enjoying my first sip of coffee, I would be deeply engrossed in the day's headlines. But over the past few years, my daily news ritual took a toll. Watching the news started to elicit feelings of anxiety, disappointment, and even outright outrage. The world's injustices, the stories of unfair treatment, the blatant wrongs—they all seemed too much. I grappled with a growing sense of responsibility, as though being informed was my civic duty, even at the expense of my mental well-being.

Here's the intriguing part: So often we mistakenly equate our anger or dismay at the world's happenings with purposeful action. We feel that our indignation, our vocal objections, somehow translate into making a difference. In truth, all that pent-up rage seldom translates into real change. It often just depletes our emotional reserves, leaving us drained and stressed.

My epiphany came during a quaint getaway with my husband. Our chosen Airbnb, nestled amid serenity, lacked the constant hum of cable news. Seizing the moment, I decided to take a complete break from my news-consuming habit. The results were nothing short of miraculous. My nights were calmer, my sleep deeper, and my days brighter. The constant weight of the world's problems, which I had shouldered unknowingly, had lifted.

But this isn't just about a personal revelation; it's deeply rooted in neuroscience. Every time we expose ourselves to distressing news or negative stimuli, our brain's amygdala—our emotional response center—springs into action. It triggers a cascade of those nasty stress hormones, notably cortisol, preparing our body for a fight-or-flight response. But when this becomes a regular event, our brain starts to rewire itself, creating stronger neural pathways associated with this stress response. In the world of neuroscience, there's a saying: "Neurons that fire together, wire together." This means that repeated exposure to distressing stimuli strengthens the neural connections that produce stress reactions.

Studies by Sherman, et al., 2009[12], and by Critcher and Dunning, 2015[13], both showed the correlation between self-affirmations and decreased stress. And Dr. Daniel Amen, a leading psychiatrist and neuroscientist, who has written extensively on the power of affirmations, states that our brains release chemicals with every thought. When we have automatic negative thoughts, the chemicals released are also negative. "Your hands get cold and wet, your muscles get tense, your heart beats faster, and your breathing becomes shallower. Additionally, the activity in your frontal and temporal lobes decreases, which negatively affects your judgment, learning, memory." Similarly, positive and kind thoughts result in positive chemicals flooding our body.[14]

By consciously choosing to limit my exposure to upsetting news, I was giving my brain a chance to reset. Over time, as those stress-triggering neural pathways are used less and less, they become weaker. In contrast, the pathways associated with relaxation, happiness, and peace get to strengthen. Essentially, we have the power to reshape our brain's wiring, emphasizing positive and calming responses over stress-induced ones.

Protecting our mental space isn't about ignorance, it's about selective awareness. In a world overflowing with information, it's essential to filter what truly deserves our attention. By guarding what we expose it to, we're not just managing stress in the present, we're also reshaping our brain's future responses, ensuring a calmer, more centered self. **Our brain is incredibly adaptable, and with intentional effort, we can steer its evolution through neuroplasticity.**

MY METHOD

What follows is a description of a "perfect day" of stress management for me. There will be days when the alarm goes off, and I can't follow through with every step. That's perfectly fine. The aim is sustained effort over time. As you immerse yourself more in the process that suits you best, you'll notice a diminishing inclination toward the fight-or-flight response characteristic of unhealthy stress. These are the steps that help me reduce stress:

1. Start the day with gratitude, meditation, and, if you believe, prayer. Whether you believe in a higher power or simply the transformative magic of a centered mind, there's a source of strength and direction available to you. If the higher power resonates with you, lean into that connection. If not, diving deep into meditation and Mindfulness practices can be just as empowering. I prefer Transcendental Meditation. I find that I can get into a meditative state easily with this method. The downside is that you need to take a course to learn the method. Taking a meditation or Mindfulness course is a great investment, but not necessary. Consider checking out apps like Insight Timer, Headspace, and Calm. They're incredible tools to help guide your meditative moments. Whenever life throws a curveball or you just need a breather, take a moment to connect, whether that's with your higher power, your inner self, or simply the rhythm of your own breath.

2. Journal. Whenever I can, I like to follow up the first step by writing down my thoughts and feelings. Whatever comes to mind. What I'm concerned about, what I'm thankful for, what I dread doing that day, and what I'm looking forward to. There's lots of research demonstrating that journaling can have significant mental health benefits, including stress reduction, improvement in mood, enhancement of self-awareness, better conflict resolution skills, and even symptom reduction in certain physical health conditions. Studies indicate that the act of expressing our thoughts and feelings in writing can provide an effective therapeutic outlet and foster an overall sense of well-being. This is the time to take an inventory of the stress you're experiencing and prepare yourself for potential stress ahead.

3. Visualize. I spend at least ten minutes a day visualizing. I love the feeling of immersing myself in happy images, and I've come to see this practice as one of prevention as I know the positive effects that visualization has on my brain (and my overall well-being).

4. Exercise. For me, exercise has always been more than just a route to physical fitness. It's my sanctuary against the daily grind, a haven where stress melts away and clarity reigns. Whenever life's pressures surge, I often find myself lacing up my sneakers and heading out, letting each step become a rhythmic mantra that calms my mind.

Here's the fascinating part: Science backs this up. Engaging in physical activity prompts our brain to release endorphins, those wonderful chemicals, the "E" in DOSE. These not only act as natural painkillers but they are also potent mood elevators. Exercising also increases the secretion of serotonin and dopamine, neurotransmitters that play pivotal roles in mood regulation and feelings of well-being.[15]

My daily goal? Hitting those steps. Each step I take is like shedding a little bit of the day's stress. I also integrate weightlifting into my regimen twice a week. The sense of achievement after lifting those weights, feeling the muscles work, is unparalleled. It grounds me, reminding me of my strength and resilience, both physically and mentally.

However, I'll be the first to admit—I'm not always perfect. There are days when deadlines loom large and responsibilities beckon, and I end up prioritizing work over my workout. Yet these instances are exceptions, not the norm. Why? Because I've experienced firsthand the difference regular exercise makes to my sleep quality. After a good workout, when my head hits the pillow, sleep envelops me in a deep, rejuvenating embrace, preparing me to face another day with zeal.

It's a holistic cycle: exercise alleviates stress, which, in turn, improves sleep, further enhancing mood and energy levels. So, while the world continues its frantic pace, I've found my rhythm to dance through the chaos. My advice? Find yours. Whether it's walking, running, lifting, or dancing—just move. Your brain and body will thank you.

5. Limit caffeine and alcohol. Do I enjoy a cup of coffee or a glass of wine? You bet I do. But both can have adverse effects on your physical and mental wellness. Not to mention too much of either exacerbates racing thoughts plus increases your blood pressure, making you feel more anxious than you would without either. And though I hate to admit it, the same goes for another one of my great loves: sugar.

6. Laugh. There are so many studies on the positive benefits of laughing out loud. According to the Mayo Clinic, laughter has short-term benefits that include increasing oxygen-rich air intake, stimulating the heart, lungs, and muscles. Laughter also releases endorphins, reducing your cortisol levels, and likewise, your stress. Laughter can also lower your blood pressure and increase circulation, relaxing your muscles and lessening the physical effects of stress on your body.[16]

Every night before I go to bed, I watch stand-up comedy on YouTube. I have a list of comedians I love. I watch fifteen minutes to a half hour, and I simply laugh. You'd be surprised by how much better you sleep when your last moments awake are spent laughing. I listen to Comedy Central and Just for Laughs comedy on Sirus XM in the car. Listening and laughing stops me from getting frustrated in traffic, and I arrive at my destination refreshed and happy.

7. Get adequate sleep. For many of us high achievers, we like to steal away hours at the beginning and end of the day to get more work done. If you're anything like the old me (the one with unhealthy stress), you've fallen asleep with a computer in your lap more than once. But getting the right amount of sleep won't slow you down—it'll only speed you up.

Sleep is incredibly beneficial to our overall well-being. In fact, next to food and water, sleep is vital to actually living. Sleep is our body's chance to rest and repair, as well as our brain's chance to consolidate all the information we took in during the day.

Mood regulation is another crucial facet of sleep. Ever notice heightened irritability or mood swings after a restless night? Sleep deprivation impairs our brain's ability to regulate emotions, leading to heightened reactions to both positive and negative stimuli. Moreover, during deep phases of our sleep cycle, our brain's waste-clearance system—the glymphatic system—becomes active, clearing away potential neurotoxins, which, if accumulated, could contribute to neurodegenerative diseases.

And then there's stress. A good night's rest keeps the stress hormone cortisol balanced, ensuring we don't dive deep into the spirals of anxiety. But the benefits don't end with mental well-being.

Sleep has a direct impact on our dietary choices too. When deprived of sleep, our body produces more ghrelin, the hunger-stimulating hormone, and reduces leptin, which signals when we're full. This imbalance not only amplifies hunger but also nudges us toward calorie-rich, unhealthy food choices. This can initiate a vicious cycle: poor dietary choices lead to fatigue, which diminishes the motivation to exercise, further exacerbating stress and negatively impacting sleep quality.

Getting adequate sleep will make you more productive during your waking hours. A few sleeping apps I recommend are ENDEL, Insight Timer, Calm, and Headspace. Insight Timer has a guided meditation for times you wake up in the night and can't fall back to sleep.

8. Find Joy. I regularly incorporate things that bring happiness into my life, such as self-care. I also look for opportunities to surround myself with things and activities I love, a few each week. I've always loved interior design, or, as I and others call it, "house porn." Scrolling through Pinterest or deciding on a paint color by pouring over color fans gives me a thrill, and we know what that does for the brain.

I'm a bit of a nerd when it comes to anything leadership, and I build in a few hours a week to read the latest theories.

I also love getting massages, so I make sure to schedule them frequently. Not only is it downtime, but it's good for my body, especially as I continue to age.

LET'S TEST YOUR STRESS

Are you curious to see where you fall in terms of healthy stress vs. unhealthy stress? It's important to note that this quiz is not a substitute for professional medical advice, diagnosis, or treatment. If you have concerns about your stress levels, it's always best to consult with a health-care provider.

For the following questions, choose the answer that most closely reflects your current reality.

I often work late or bring work home.

Almost never (0 points)
Occasionally (1 point)
Often (2 points)
Almost always (3 points)

My personal life often takes a back seat to my work commitments.

Almost never (0 points)
Occasionally (1 point)
Often (2 points)
Almost always (3 points)

I often take time for self-care and things that bring me joy.

Almost always (0 points)
Often (1 point)
Occasionally (2 points)
Almost never (3 points)

My goals and responsibilities often leave me feeling overwhelmed.

Almost never (0 points)
Occasionally (1 point)
Often (2 points)
Almost always (3 points)

I often feel the negative physical effects of stress, including fatigue and headaches.

Almost never (0 points)
Occasionally (1 point)
Often (2 points)
Almost always (3 points)

My current achievements and success make me feel . . .

Completely satisfied (0 points)
Mostly satisfied (1 point)
Somewhat dissatisfied (2 points)
Highly dissatisfied (3 points)

I often feel inadequate when I compare myself to others.

Almost never (0 points)
Occasionally (1 point)
Often (2 points)
Almost always (3 points)

My self-worth is often defined by my work accomplishments.

Almost never (0 points)
Occasionally (1 point)
Often (2 points)
Almost always (3 points)

I often feel anxious due to the pressure to be my best.

Almost never (0 points)
Occasionally (1 point)
Often (2 points)
Almost always (3 points)

I usually maintain a work–life balance.

Almost always (0 points)
Often (1 point)
Occasionally (2 points)
Almost never (3 points)

SCORING:

0–9 points: Impressive! You've managed to strike a healthy balance when it comes to stress.

10–18 points: Not too bad! You haven't found that balance yet, but with a few changes to your priorities, you'll get there.

19–27 points: Time to make some changes! Your stress is at a high level, and you may benefit from some professional support to help you manage it.

28–30 points: Stress overload! Your responses suggest that you may be living with chronic stress. I highly recommend you take notice and consult a mental health professional.

Were you surprised by your stress score? If you'd like to decrease your score, you must identify the areas in your life where you can eliminate the long-term, nagging stress that doesn't serve you well.

I had a client once who was constantly stressed out. Let's call her Susie. Susie was a C-suite powerhouse, orchestrating success in her corporate life while cherishing her time at home with her husband and two children. But a realization dawned on her: she was *only* stressed out at home. It wasn't the family or the job; it was something deeper, something linked to the environment itself.

Working with me helped her identify that she was experiencing environmental stress, stemming from the lack of a personal space within her home. Susie decided to claim a space of her own. She bought a pre-manufactured "She Shed" and poured her creativity into transforming it into a sanctuary. Filled with her favorite books, soft lighting, and cozy furniture, it became her escape. Every evening she would steal away for twenty to thirty minutes in her private oasis. The change was immediate, and Susie's stress levels leveled out. Susie's "She Shed" wasn't just a structure—it was a symbol of her strength, self-awareness, and love for herself.

Think about the times, places, and people who cause you the most chronic stress and write them down.

TIMES: ....

....

....

PLACES: ....

....

....

PEOPLE: ....

....

....

Do you notice any patterns? ....

....

....

If you finally conquer your stress, be forewarned: it may make you feel like you've "lost your edge." Without that constant anxiety, you won't feel like yourself. But the cost of remaining where you are now is too great—we're talking about the physical health of your body—it's not worth it. There is a better way.

Out of the stress-minimizing actions mentioned in this chapter, I want to challenge you to start with implementing just one. Set a goal for how long you'd like to try it out, giving it at least fourteen days. Then come back here and answer the following questions (set a reminder on your phone or calendar now to check back—we high achievers can get distracted):

- Which action did you choose?

- Did you stick to it?

- Retake the Stress quiz.

- Did your score change or remain the same?

FROM STRESS TO BURNOUT

Many high achievers follow the same path to burnout. We start out our lives as shameless, unapologetic kids with a sense of adventure and spirit. We believe anything is possible. And because we're imaginative, inquisitive, and determined, it is. But then it happens. Inevitably, we experience failure or rejection. We don't make the team. We are left out of the friend group. Our parents' divorce. In response to our perceived failure, we subconsciously decide that on our own, we simply are not good enough. There is something fundamentally wrong with us that we must overcome.

This is what I call the ego-protection zone. In our ego-protection zone, we become performers. Almost caricatures of who we really are. For example, when I was a kid, I wasn't a great speller. My mother's well-intentioned attempts to help me study for spelling tests often ended in stress for both of us as my test results fell short of expectations. Over time, this self-perception of incompetence took root, becoming a protective shield against the fear of failure. I had convinced myself that I was simply "bad at English"—that I was bad at grammar and spelling and wasn't a good writer and this belief shaped my academic experience. I couldn't be disappointed with my test results if I believed I was inherently bad at English.

However, a remarkable twist of fate occurred when I reached grade 10. To my astonishment, I found myself placed in the advanced English class alongside the smart kids. The initial shock of this unexpected placement left me anticipating the moment when the principal would storm into our classroom, announcing that a grave mistake had been made, and I was, indeed, in the wrong class. I braced myself for the humiliation and embarrassment that would surely follow, all while trying to make myself as inconspicuous as possible to avoid the teacher's attention.

After a few weeks, a gradual realization began to dawn on me. Maybe I really did belong there. Instead of floundering, I thrived in this challenging environment. I discovered a newfound passion for literature, delving into Shakespearean works with enthusiasm and writing essays from the depths of my heart. This experience shattered the self-imposed limitations I had carried for so long.

We enter our ego-protection zone, and for many of us, we never come out. Why? Because we feel safe there. No one can hurt us because we've already made up our minds that we have failed. To make up for our "lack," we overcompensate in other areas. In *every* other area.

Because ego-protection is a subconscious decision, it's also what is called a limiting belief. Limiting beliefs are insidious. They are poisonous. They fester. And though they stay under the surface, undetected, they require a great deal of energy and time to manage. Because we're high achievers, if we feel inadequate in any way, we try to outperform our "deficiency." We tell ourselves that once we prove ourselves, we are immune from pain or embarrassment. Our achievements become the masks we wear, hiding our insecurities from the people around us.

These feelings of "not-enoughness" often play out as ambition and determination. We're even affirmed for them! We're told that we're driven. That we have goals. That we're capable, dependable, and hard working. We get so caught up in the busyness, the accolades, and the achievements that we are distracted from dealing with the issue(s) at hand. We spend so much of our time subconsciously trying to overcome our perceived inadequacies that we move from accomplishment to accomplishment without taking a breath. There's no time to rest. There's more work to be done. We're not there yet. We have to keep going, keep pushing, and keep moving forward. We feel good about ourselves in the limelight, when we check a box or get it right, but that feeling becomes increasingly fleeting. It's not enough.

And if we're honest with ourselves, we're not happy. It's a cycle that's draining and painful. We feel uninspired. We feel trapped. We feel *exhausted*.

I'm not saying having goals is a bad thing. Quite the opposite, in fact. But there comes a point in every high achiever's journey when goals and benchmarks and checked boxes take control. They become more important than anything else. And until we attain them, we don't feel good about ourselves anymore. So, I'm here to ask you, when is enough, enough?

BURNOUT

Does this scenario sound familiar to you?

You're in back-to-back meetings or calls all day long. You put on a smile, you say the right things, you close the deals. As the clock strikes closer to 5 p.m., you open your computer to a mountain of emails. As you try to delete any that don't need your attention, your door opens. It's a team member. They want to chat about weekend plans or about an upcoming project. You nod appropriately, but your mind is really on your inbox and how desperately you want to sift through it before leaving. To no avail. By the time the team member leaves, it's time to pick the kids up from daycare. You get home, order takeout, and try to focus on your kids while scrolling through emails and texts to "finish" work for the day. Homework, laundry, dishes, and baths follow. It's late now. But quiet. So, you open your laptop and confront your emails again. Only somehow, because you weren't paying attention for all of two hours, the number in your inbox has increased significantly. You spend the next hour or two narrowing them down before falling exhausted into bed. But as you lie there, you can't sleep. Your mind is back to the call you had earlier that day and the client who just wasn't ready to close.

I should have said this . . .

I shouldn't have said that . . .

I'll give them a call tomorrow . . .

Or maybe an email . . .

And then you're thinking about the mountain of emails you still need to return.

You haven't exercised in weeks. You can't remember the last time you had a social outing. And your diet has become suspiciously similar to the one you had in college when your metabolism was a *lot* better. The next thing you know, the alarm clock is screaming. It's time to wake up and do it all again.

You're burning the candle at both ends. Heck, your candle is nothing more than a smoky flicker. You feel like your life is a sad song on repeat. You don't know how to get out of the rut you're in. But you do want out. Only that would mean giving up. That would mean failure. That would mean you're a loser. So you button your blouse, drop the kids at school, and walk back to your desk like the professional you are.

You, my friend, are either on the brink of, or are in full-blown, job burnout, which can lead to serious consequences.

It can affect your physical, mental, and social health. But it doesn't just happen—it gradually builds over time.

CHASING THE EXTRAORDINARY: A RECIPE FOR BURNOUT

The World Health Organization, in 2019, officially recognized burnout as an occupational phenomenon, calling it "a syndrome conceptualized as resulting from chronic workplace stress that has not been successfully managed."[17] While factors contributing to burnout are multifaceted, the relentless chase for an extraordinary life undoubtedly plays a role. High achievers often find themselves in a perpetual loop of dissatisfaction, always yearning for more.

High achievers tend to be people who are always "on." And according to a 2014 study by Monster.com (the online job site), 61 percent of employees have experienced physical illness related to their "on-ness," and work-related stress.[18]

In a 2021 report on work and well-being, the American Psychological Association found that 71 percent of workers admitted to feeling stressed during their workday, with 59 percent feeling the negative effects of long-term stress.[19]

High achievers are the most common victims of burnout, especially at the executive level where the spotlight is particularly bright. There are a few reasons we find ourselves among this group of burned-out, exhausted, non-inspired workers.

1. Low Self-esteem

Though they may exude confidence, high achievers grapple with fluctuating self-esteem; they cannot recognize the worth others attribute to them.

2. Self-doubt

They set unreasonably high standards for themselves, tending to focus on the negatives and overlooking achievements. This can help personal growth in the short term, but left unabated, it can have a detrimental effect on the individual.

3. People-pleasing

People with low self-confidence often try to please others and overwork to meet expectations, leading to boundary issues and an unrelenting inner critic.

4. Overthinking

High achievers constantly think and rethink things because of their need to perform at a high level. They find it hard to switch off and are usually preoccupied with their long to-do list.

5. Lack of Boundaries

High achievers often struggle to create and maintain boundaries. With that, we are more apt to ignore our personal needs and bend our boundaries in order to oblige others. This can come in the form of saying yes to something we don't want to do or working incessantly to reach a certain level of quality.

Chasing goals at all costs can lead to burnout. This is particularly true when the goals don't resonate with us or bring happiness. An important step in avoiding burnout is to take an honest look at why we're intently chasing our goals—or are fulfilling our self-imposed obligations—in the first place.

REFLECTION

- Do my goals inspire me or drain me of all my energy?
- Do I feel like once I reach a certain level, my life will be better?
- Do my goals feel more like obligations?
- Do I find myself practicing "numbing" habits in order to reach this goal (spending, drinking, using prescription medication, etc.)?
- Is this goal something I want to accomplish for me, or is it something I want to accomplish for someone else?

CHAPTER 3:
THE DOUBLE-EDGED SWORD OF BEING A HIGH ACHIEVER

Being the "best" is not necessarily the best place to be, especially when it comes at a cost.
–Diane von Fürstenberg

While outstanding accomplishments reflect our impressive motivation and resilience, there are two sides to every coin—or two sides to every blade. Our strengths can sometimes work against us, and we can unconsciously harbor self-sabotaging habits. Being a high achiever is, to be sure, a double-edged sword. In fact, *The Double-Edged Sword of Being a High Achiever* was the title of this book when I first started writing it!

The goal of this chapter is to help you identify the dull edge of that sword—the edge that does not serve you; the edge that threatens the very best in you. But it's an edge that, with the right amount of work, you can sharpen to make you happier, more effective, and at peace with yourself.

Many of you reading need to hear this: High-achieving women, you are powerhouses. You've conquered insurmountable odds, navigated the toughest terrains, and yet, like all humans, you've realized that sometimes the hardest journey is the one within. The leap from negative bias to positive optimism requires not just the desire to change but also the discipline and effort to make that shift. But why (despite knowing the benefits) do some of us hesitate or even resist this transformation? Why do we question it?

It's counterintuitive to think negative behaviors and patterns can be beneficial. However, sometimes, our psyche holds on to them because they serve a purpose, even if that purpose isn't ultimately for our highest good. Negative emotions, beliefs, and biases can act as protective barriers, giving us a (false) sense of safety or justification.

DULL EDGE #1: THE FEAR OF CHANGE

The future, with all its possibilities, can be incredibly intimidating. Especially when it means parting with familiar, albeit limiting, beliefs. For high achievers, the fear of the unknown might paradoxically feel more daunting because we're used to being in control, and uncertainty challenges that control.

Take the story of my friend, Darlene. A successful chief human resources officer, her accomplishments would make anyone's jaw drop. Yet when it came to her ex-husband, it was as though all her empowerment vanished. She would routinely drive by his house, even his place of work. The hurt she believed he caused her consumed her every thought.

One day while we were on a drive, she brought him up again. In a moment of exasperation, I asked her if she genuinely wanted to stop thinking of him. I was taken aback when she simply said no. That's when it hit me. Holding on to that resentment, anger, and obsession gave her something—a distraction, a sense of self-righteousness, or maybe even a reason to not move on. Whatever it was, in her eyes, it felt safer and more comforting than letting go.

Happiness and contentment often feel like they're at the mercy of others and our circumstances, but this belief actually gives away our personal power. The truth is, our happiness is shaped more by our own thoughts and feelings than by external factors. When we understand we control our inner world, we no longer let others or situations dictate our joy. By taking charge of our thoughts and emotions, we take back the reins of our happiness. This simple shift in perspective is a powerful step toward a more fulfilled and self-empowered life.

Change, even the good kind, demands effort. Staying in your comfort zone, even if it's filled with self-doubt and negativity, is . . . well, comfortable. Not trying to change also offers a reprieve from potential disappointment. If you never try, you never fail, right? The problem is, clinging to the past or even clinging to the present can create a negative bias within us.

Negative biases and behaviors can provide an odd sense of identity. For Darlene, her fixation on her ex-husband, though unhealthy, became a significant part of who she was. Letting go might feel like losing a piece of oneself. Humans are creatures of habit. Even if a behavior is self-destructive, the sheer familiarity of it offers comfort. We understand its boundaries, its triggers, and its outcomes. Altering these behaviors means venturing into the unknown, and that uncertainty can be unsettling.

Over time, certain behaviors, even if negative, become entwined with our sense of self. "I'm always the procrastinator" or "I just have bad luck in relationships" might be narratives we tell ourselves. The first step in changing this type of self-sabotage is to recognize it. Once you're able to see the behavior and its results as negative, it's easier to stop it—although altering these behaviors challenges our long-held beliefs and forces us to redefine our identity, which can be both empowering and anxiety-inducing.

While the journey from a negative mindset to a positive one is demanding, it is also immensely rewarding. Recognizing the unconscious reasons you might be clinging to negatively is the first step. Once you understand, you can gently, bit by bit, begin to reframe, reassess, and ultimately rebuild.

DULL EDGE #2: FEAR OF BEING "ORDINARY"

In today's fast-paced world, dominated by glossy magazine covers, social media perfection, and the curated lives of the rich and famous, the pressure to lead an extraordinary life is overwhelming. And for the modern high-achieving woman, these expectations can be both a motivator and a dangerous pitfall.

The Illusion of the Extraordinary Life: The Weight of High Achievement

Oprah Winfrey, an icon of success and inspiration, has graced numerous magazine covers, each touting the principles of leading an extraordinary life. One particular article quoted her saying that living a happy, successful life boils down to four things: "feeling more confident, finding your purpose, making other people feel special, and living and working with intention." While such sentiments are surely positive, the weight of achieving all these can be too much.

Consider this: In 2020, among top-selling magazines, over 30 percent featured cover stories related to living an "exceptional" or "extraordinary" life. The underlying message? Ordinary isn't enough.[20]

The Competitiveness Conundrum

Competition, especially for those who are intrinsically competitive, can be a driving force. It's not just about competing with others; for many high achievers, the real competition is with oneself. Striving for more, pushing boundaries, and relentless self-improvement can lead to significant achievements. However, it's essential to question the cost of this incessant drive.

The societal pressure to live extraordinarily implies that just existing, loving, and experiencing life is not enough. This can erode the happiness and contentment derived from simple pleasures and small successes.

Social Media: Amplifying the Illusion

While magazine covers have been around for decades, social media, with its ubiquitous presence, amplifies the pressures tenfold. High achievers, exposed to a constant stream of others' achievements, often feel the need to "keep up." Research from a 2019 study revealed that nearly 60 percent of women felt inadequate or lacked in some way after scrolling through social media platforms.[21]

Fear of Success

We fear both success and failure. Success is a trigger for the impostor syndrome. A lack of "deservedness." Fear of envy. Fear of change. Fear of not belonging in a family. Fear of the next steps. Being the only successful person in your family is a lot of pressure. Underlying beliefs can cause fear. It drives fear.

DULL EDGE #3: FEELING LIKE AN IMPOSTOR

Impostor Syndrome—a shadowy figure lurking in the corners of our mind, whispering words of self-doubt, undermining our achievements, and convincing us that we're mere pretenders on the grand stage of life. We've all felt the sting of this inner critic at some point, that gnawing suspicion that we're not quite good enough, that our success is the result of sheer luck or the kindness of others rather than our own abilities.

Unmasking the Silent Saboteur

I was catching up with the president of a large international ad agency over lunch when our conversation turned to our career high points. When I asked about his proudest moment, his energy changed. He leaned in and confided, "I rarely feel proud. I'm usually too worried someone will find out I'm not as good as they think I am."

That a person of his stature and success could feel this way was surprising—and enlightening. If such accomplished individuals grapple with these feelings, it's understandable that many others do too. The causes for impostor syndrome are varied, from perfectionism to fear of failure to a lack of internal validation, just to name a few.

Feeling like an impostor is not only mentally draining but also exhausting. It can gnaw away at your self-confidence, even in the face of evidence that you're skilled and quite successful. However, take solace in the fact you are not alone. Most of us, regardless of our accomplishments or status, have felt like an impostor at one point or another.

A significant number of individuals who experience impostor syndrome come from families that highly value success. Parents who oscillate between giving excessive praise and criticism can elevate the likelihood of fraudulent feelings in the future. Furthermore, societal demands can exacerbate the situation.

Though high achievers are typically confident people, we still battle impostor syndrome. I think many of us, deep down, try to overcompensate for our insecurities by working overtime to prove to ourselves and others we are capable and deserve to be where we are.

The problems arise when "proving ourselves" becomes our long-term motivation. Bad habits, unhealthy patterns, and fatigue will eventually settle in. In addition, impostor syndrome is miserable. You constantly feel like a fraud—like you're wearing a mask. You are afraid if anyone were to know the authentic version of you, you would be rejected. Maybe even fired. You don't have to live that way!

FIVE SIGNS OF IMPOSTOR SYNDROME

There are five tell-tale signs of impostor syndrome. See how many ring true for you:

1. They worry others expect too much of them.

Not surprisingly, someone with impostor syndrome often worries others have too high expectations of them. They often think they're not as smart or talented as their superiors view them and worry constantly about being found out. This fear causes them constant stress as they often seek (positive) feedback and long for validation from others.

2. They find it difficult to celebrate their success.

While achievement typically boosts self-confidence, individuals with impostor syndrome experience heightened self-doubt following success. Each new accomplishment amplifies their fear of being exposed as a fraud. Instead of feeling validated by their achievements, they feel as though they need to work harder to maintain the illusion of competence, perpetuating a sense of inadequacy.

3. They rarely feel content with where they are in their job, their life.

Despite their accomplishments, individuals who experience impostor syndrome often struggle to find satisfaction in their work. And this feeling of inadequacy may also lead them to resist opportunities for career advancement, as they feel they are already working so hard to keep up the facade. This reluctance to pursue higher positions is often rooted in a deep-seated fear of failure, as well as a belief that they lack the necessary skills and abilities to succeed. Consequently, people with impostor syndrome may find themselves feeling stuck in their current roles, unable to pursue their full potential.

4. They are uncomfortable with self-promotion.

Those with impostor syndrome experience both a paralyzing fear of failure and terror of success. They strive to prove their worth, but their self-doubt leads them to believe they are undeserving of praise and an increased salary. Because they secretly doubt their self-worth, they require confirmation from others and usually avoid asking for their actual worth at work. This results in them feeling stagnant in their job as they compare themselves to others who are making more or advancing faster.

5. They are perfectionists who lack self-confidence.

People with impostor syndrome tend to focus all their energy on performing within their designated roles with excessive detail in an effort to avoid constructive criticism, which they usually take personally. Consequently, they may spend more time on projects and work overtime to get something just right in the need to garner positive feedback and quell their insecure inner voice.

FIVE TYPES OF IMPOSTOR SYNDROME

In my experience, there are generally five types of "impostors" when it comes to impostor syndrome. Identifying which one (or ones) you identify with most will help you break out of the impostor syndrome to embrace your strengths and improve your mental health. Do any of these reflect you?

WONDER WOMAN

If you identify as a Wonder Woman, you may already believe you are not as competent as your colleagues, causing you to overexert yourself to prove your worth. This tendency to overachieve can lead to an addiction to external validation rather than a genuine love for the work. In an effort to counteract your feelings of inadequacy, you may work longer hours than your peers and struggle to relax outside of work.

Are you a Wonder Woman?

- Do you seek external validation to feel that you are worthy and deserving?
- Do you take criticism personally rather than constructively?
- Do you find it hard to say no and set boundaries?
- Are you a workaholic and is it affecting your personal and family life?

THE PERFECTIONIST

If you identify as a Perfectionist, you may hold yourself, and others, to an unrealistic and extremely high standard. You hate making mistakes and ruminate over them, even long after they've passed. You frequently work excessive hours, often micromanaging projects to ensure success.

Are you a Perfectionist?

- Do you hold yourself to an extremely high standard?
- Do you find yourself dwelling on minor errors after a presentation?
- Do you tend to focus more on your failures than your successes?
- Do you require perfection and find anything less unacceptable?

THE KNOW-IT-ALL

You may not like to be known as a know-it-all, as it may make you feel like you need to have all the answers and you feel the pressure to live up to such a high standard. You might be called the "subject matter expert" in a certain field or the "go-to person" in a particular project. If you are asked a question and don't have the answer, you feel like a fraud or feel shame. You find yourself reading more books, taking more courses, and getting more certificates to ensure you won't feel that way again. You may even hold yourself back from going for promotions because you never quite feel qualified enough.

Are you a Know-It-All?

- Do you shy away from applying to job postings unless you meet every single educational requirement?

- Are you constantly seeking out trainings or certifications because you think you need to improve your skills in order to succeed?

- Even if you've been in your role for some time, can you relate to feeling like you still don't know "enough"?

- Do you shudder when someone says you're an expert?

THE LONER

You may identify as a Loner if you prefer to work alone because you don't want to share credit for a job well done or risk others diluting your success. You rarely ask others for help because you don't want to be seen as incompetent and would rather do extra research and work longer hours to achieve your desired outcome. Even if you do accept help, or get guidance to improve, you may question your own competence.

Are you a Loner?

- Do you prefer to work alone than in teams?

- Do you prefer to do something yourself rather than delegate an important task?

- Do you spend copious amounts of time researching a new topic or working on a project instead of asking for help?

- Do you feel undeserving of credit if you require help with something?

THE INTELLECTUAL

The Intellectual is similar to being a perfectionist. You have a strong desire to know all the facts and information related to a task, not just getting it perfect. If you don't have all the information, you become frustrated with yourself. Perhaps you started a new job in a technical field, but you aren't as technical. You feel frustrated that it's taking you longer to grasp the information. You may start avoiding situations like meetings or managers until you feel like you know everything. This is because your self-worth is based on being an intellectual.

Are you an Intellectual?

- Are you considered the "smart one" in your family or group of friends?
- Did you perform well academically and are you trying to apply the same level of achievement to your work now?
- Do you struggle with ambiguity in projects and become stressed when there are gray areas?
- Did you find that things came naturally to you in the past, but now you find that it's not working that way anymore?

Which one of the five categories do you identify with the most? You may have two that you are torn between—that would not be uncommon. Here are the specific recommendations I would make for each "type" of impostor:

Wonder Woman:

The weight of embodying "Wonder Woman" isn't a badge of honor, it's an albatross. No one can perpetually sustain such standards. The fall, when it comes, can be daunting.

Yet the real strength lies not in donning the armor but in understanding that vulnerability doesn't equal weakness. Real power resides in the inner voice that uplifts and reassures rather than the external affirmations that merely placate.

One of the simplest and most profound methods to start bolstering this internal voice is maintaining a "Positivity File." Every commendation, every congratulatory note, every laudatory message—save them. On days when doubt looms large, this file serves as a tangible reminder of your worth.

Reinforce this with generous doses of positive self-talk. The voice inside your head should be your best cheerleader and biggest fan. When faced with criticism or feedback, pause. Breathe. Understand that this isn't an attack on your person but merely a pointer toward growth. Not beating yourself up when you make a mistake is a way of showing self-love. Self-love is not about self-indulgence or being narcissistic. It's about treating yourself with the same compassion, understanding, and patience you'd offer to someone you deeply care about. It's acknowledging that you, as much as anyone in the universe, deserve love and respect.

I once had the privilege of working with a young, award-winning creative director. On the outside, she exuded confidence, but she constantly sought validation from her superior. As we navigated this, it became evident that her "Wonder Woman" facade was a shield against self-doubt. Together, we explored ways for her to derive validation from within. She began recording her achievements, however small, and reflecting on them regularly. This act of introspection gradually diminished her dependence on external approval.

How can you fill the validation chasm?

Self-reflection: Take the time to regularly record your achievements, big and small, in a notebook and review them daily. You will come to see all the positives and begin to believe how great you really are. Take a look at your qualities, not just your accomplishments. You're more than what you achieve: think about how creative, logical, or tough you may be. Listing your qualities and values help you validate how fabulous you are.

Mindfulness: Whenever you feel overwhelmed, engage in Mindfulness practices to ground you in the present. By focusing on your thoughts and feelings in a nonjudgmental way, you'll begin to see things as they truly are rather than how you've perceived them to be.

Positive Self-talk: Recognize when you begin your self-doubt talk and squash that negative inner voice. Remind yourself of your achievements and positives and regularly give yourself encouragement.

Set Boundaries: Overworking often stems from the need to constantly prove oneself. Recognize when you're pushing beyond your limits and evaluate the reasons behind it.

In embracing your humanity, remember that you're not defined by infallibility. Mistakes, hiccups, and stumbles are inherent to the journey. The crux is not in sidestepping them but in how you rise after them. Your brain is malleable and will adapt to the narrative you feed it. Feed it empowerment, resilience, and self-belief.

The Perfectionist:

Many women have the belief that doing everything perfectly will shield them from criticism or doubt, which is a heavy burden to bear. Every slight misstep is magnified, becoming a potential revelation of their perceived inadequacies. And the irony is palpable: using perfectionism to combat feelings of impostor syndrome is counterproductive. The very strategy you believe is your armor can be your weakness. The precious hours and mental energy expended in the quest for flawlessness could instead be directed toward truly meaningful and fruitful endeavors.

It's essential to understand the dangers of this perfectionism trap. For those paralyzed by the thought of not executing tasks perfectly, it's helpful to confront these fears directly, and just take the first step! Taking that initial step, regardless of the looming specter of potential mistakes, is often the hardest but most crucial. Additionally, shifting focus from achieving absolute perfection to appreciating the journey and progress can offer much-needed perspective. Instead of being consumed by what wasn't achieved, relishing the milestones reached can be immensely gratifying.

Embracing imperfections is equally vital. After all, it's often our mistakes and the lessons they teach that catalyze genuine innovation and growth.

The Know-It-All:

The belief that you're perpetually falling short of expertise, despite evidence to the contrary, can be paralyzing. Constantly chasing the notion that acquiring just "one more skill" or "one more degree" will solidify your status as an expert can be a self-sabotaging endeavor. This endless pursuit only fuels the impostor syndrome, trapping you in a cycle where you never feel quite "enough." No amount of external validation can replace inner confidence; there's always another mountain to climb, and if you're always looking upward, you'll never recognize how high you've already ascended.

But as someone who has navigated this terrain, I've learned it's less about the total accumulation of knowledge and more about trusting in the knowledge we already possess. To begin, redefine expertise. Expertise isn't about knowing everything, it's about dedication, continuous learning, and applying our knowledge effectively. No one can know it all.

Embracing your unique perspective is another pivotal step. Your experiences, insights, and journey provide a lens no one else possesses. Instead of getting caught up in comparisons, trust in your unique narrative and value the insights only you can bring.

Moreover, it's crucial to remember that every expert, at some point, was a novice. Every time you feel as if you don't know enough, think about how much you've learned since you started. Chart your growth, and soon enough, you'll see the expert you've become.

Errors, setbacks, and lapses are intrinsic to any learning curve. Normalize them. They don't invalidate your expertise but rather reinforce your commitment to growth. It's less about the absence of mistakes and more about resilience and adaptability in the face of them.

One effective practice I recommend is to document your achievements. Create a tangible testament to your progress and competencies. Reviewing this periodically can offer a much-needed reminder of your growth and capability, especially on days clouded by doubt. This is repeated for each archetype because it's an important antidote to the impostor feelings.

Equally, challenge any negative self-talk head-on. Interrogate its roots: Is it fact-based or merely a manifestation of unfounded fears?

Last, remember that the pursuit of knowledge is a lifelong journey. Feeling out of depth occasionally is not a sign of inadequacy but an indication of growth and boundary-pushing. It's about framing these moments not as shortcomings but as opportunities for further enrichment. Trust in your knowledge and your journey.

The Loner:

For those who identify with the Loner archetype, there's an internal struggle tied to vulnerability. Many might resonate with the adage, "It's better to remain silent and be thought a fool than to speak and remove all doubt." But in reality, withholding questions or keeping ideas to oneself can actually hamper growth and feed the impostor syndrome. It's crucial to remember that everyone, no matter how seasoned or knowledgeable, once started from a place of not knowing. There's strength in seeking clarity.

Being brave enough to ask questions or request help doesn't expose inadequacy but showcases a dedication to understanding and growth. One of the most effective ways to combat feelings of being an impostor is to build a personal arsenal of knowledge and skills. Acknowledge them, reflect on them, and recognize their value.

Seek out teamwork opportunities: Look for chances to work on projects with other people, then view the team's success as your own. Being a team player is an important skill that employers value, and working together can increase efficiency and provide more room for creativity and work–life balance. Over time, this will help reframe your perspective from an isolated individual lacking in capabilities to a competent professional who, like everyone else, benefits from the collective wisdom of a community.

The Intellectual:

We are so much more than what we know or how smart we are or what we've accomplished. Think about it: When someone praises you solely for your intelligence or accomplishments, do you ever feel a tad bit empty? This is because while our achievements are a part of who we are, they aren't the whole story. There's a depth to us that goes beyond our degrees, job titles, or accolades. There's a spirit, a heart, and unique experiences that shape us.

One of the exercises I frequently introduce in my coaching sessions is the "What else are you?" exercise. Begin by stating a known strength or achievement and then ask yourself, "What else am I?" So, if you start with "I'm smart," then follow it with "And what else?" Maybe you're compassionate, a loving parent, a dedicated friend, or a person with a keen sense of humor. By repeatedly asking "What else?" you delve deeper into the layers of your identity.

By acknowledging the wonderful multifaceted person you are, you'll be more likely to gain confidence in your different aspects and not put all your value into your intelligence. Recognizing that being smart is only part of who you are takes the pressure off knowing everything all the time. Embracing this fuller, holistic view of ourselves can ground us, making those impostors' voices grow fainter.

High achievers, those who always strive to reach the pinnacle of success, often hold themselves to incredibly lofty standards. If they fall short of these (sometimes unfairly high) expectations, they may feel inadequate, even if they're doing better than those around them. It's this gap between self-expectation and reality that can sometimes fuel feelings of being an impostor.

DULL EDGE #4: ECHOES OF DOUBT: CONFRONTING NEGATIVE SELF-TALK

Negative self-talk often sits at the intersection of personal fears and societal expectations, particularly the dread of disappointing others. This harmful internal dialogue manifests as a defensive mechanism that attempts to cushion the prospect of failure or criticism by rehearsing it privately first. Stemming from the desire to meet the standards set by others, whether family, friends, or professional peers, it inadvertently magnifies our shortcomings and underestimates our capabilities. This overemphasis on potential failure rather than recognizing personal achievements fosters an environment of self-doubt, resulting in a perpetual state of self-criticism. In addressing this, it's important to cultivate self-awareness, intercept this negative pattern, and replace it with affirmations of our worth and strengths.

Negative self-talk is intrinsically embedded into our culture. It's everywhere. You turn on your TV or log in to LinkedIn and you are immediately bombarded with the subtle message that you simply do not measure up. You've got a job? There's someone higher up than you are. You've got a family? There's someone whose family is happier than yours. You've got friends? Nope. This is what *real* friendship looks like. The message is clear: You are not enough.

But we high achievers don't need culture to tell us that, do we? We have been thinking that for years. For basically our entire lives. We may not have been cognizant, but subconsciously, we've thought it.

In a sense, we are all products of our childhood programming. What do I mean by programming? From the moment we are born, everything we have seen, everything we have heard, and everything we have thought is temporarily recorded by our brain. The messages we received that were repeated most frequently are actually wired into our brain. Those repeated messages are called "programs." And the more our programs are repeated, the stronger they are wired into our brain.

Our brains are designed to act on the strongest programs they receive as though they are true—whether they're actually true or not. The part of your brain that stores the programs you receive cannot differentiate between fact and fiction. So, when we program our mind to believe something through a lot of negative self-talk and self-doubt, it rings true. As Henry Ford so aptly said, "Whether you believe you can or you can't, you're right."

We're all holding on to inaccurate programs we are likely not even aware of. And, more importantly, we're all acting on inaccurate programs we are not aware of.

The thoughts you have toward yourself and how you talk to yourself are products of your programming. Your strongest programs will become your most prominent thoughts. Because of neuroplasticity, your brain is designed to rewire itself over and over again throughout your life. If you do have negative programs (we all do), you can change that by working to rewire your brain.

Negative self-talk is a problem—especially for us high achievers. Why? Because we can be harder on ourselves than the average person. And the way we speak to ourselves and think about ourselves directly affects our moods, habits, and mental health. We will work ourselves into oblivion because 1) we love to work, and 2) we only feel affirmed through our work. The only way we know to silence the negative self-talk is to work more. But work as a sole means of affirmation will lead to unhealthy patterns and, eventually, burnout.

What is negative self-talk?

- Anything you think or say about yourself that focuses on your negative qualities and not your positive qualities
- Anything you think or say that comes from the perspective of what *won't* work and not what *might* work
- Anything you think or say that leans into your fears and not into your strengths

- Anything you think or say that sees the world through a lens of worst-case scenario

- Anything you think or say that is problem-oriented and not solution-oriented

- Anything you think or say that limits you from being or achieving realistic goals

- Anything you think or say that leaves no room for hope or improvement

It may be easy for us to point out how negative talk sounds when it comes from other people. But how about when it comes from us? Do you find yourself thinking or saying . . .

I'm so stupid.

I can't do anything right.

Why should I even try?

It's just going to be one of those days.

Nothing ever works out for me.

I just can't do this anymore.

I'm so fat.

Life sucks.

My kids are driving me crazy.

I can't handle this.

It's just no use.

I'm not cut out for this.

I never have enough time to get everything done.

I can't get organized.

This is impossible.

No one likes me.

Everything I touch turns to shit.

Each and every time we repeat these negative things to ourselves, we're rewiring our brain or reinforcing existing unhealthy programs. It's not just psychobabble, it's real neurotransmitters at work.

"I'm just hard on myself," you might say. "It's how I motivate myself." If you think that, then you need to find another source of motivation. Because negative self-talk does nothing but set you up for failure. **That's all negative self-talk is—a prediction of future failure. When we wire our brains to fail, they'll do just that.**

Unfortunately, we're all guilty of negative self-talk. My clients tend to fall into one of these three categories:

Stage One Negative Self-Talker. This person has generally been positive throughout their life but has experienced some sort of trauma. Maybe they've experienced something negative at work, like they were passed over for a promotion or their boss gave them a bad review. Or maybe they've experienced something negative at home; perhaps their partner left or was unfaithful. Or they are struggling to manage a work–life balance. Whatever the case, a negative situation has occurred and the negative thoughts have followed in kind: *Nothing good ever happens to me. This is too much. Maybe I'm not cut out for this. I suck. Life sucks.*

If this is you, you're smiling less, focusing on the downside of all situations, and you're beginning to lose trust that things will work out. You're more critical of yourself and others, and you are slowly becoming suspicious or paranoid.

This is a critical stage to catch yourself in because your brain hasn't yet been rewired to a new program.

Stage Two Negative Self-Talker. This person has been practicing negative self-talk for a while. It hasn't been their lifestyle, but it's been their habit lately. This person has already missed a few of life's opportunities because they have developed a victim mentality. The world around them seems unfair and everyone is out to "get" them. Their default is to see the glass half-full, and to point it out too. One thing I've noticed about this stage of negative self-talk is that the people are usually bad listeners. Why? Because they've already made up their mind about what is true. They're often fatigued, filled with dread, and self-focused.

If this is you, you're probably miserable. Maybe not on the surface, but deep down, you're in pain. And guess what? You're making the people around you miserable too. You aren't happy with your life or with yourself. You want things to be different, but you don't have hope that anything can change for the better.

Stage Three Negative Self-Talker: I can't say I've ever coached a stage three negative self-talker, but I've known them. I think most high achievers stop themselves before they get to this point, but I'm sure there are some of us out there. This person is seldom happy, is selfish, ignores the needs of others, and has lost all trust in themselves and the world around them. This person is never fun or uplifting. They're never hopeful. And they're often fatalistic and swing from crisis to crisis.

If this is you, I'm sorry. I want you to know that life is better than it feels right now. I would encourage you to reach out to a professional to get the help you need to rewire your brain and reset your programs.

Cognitive Behavioral Therapy (CBT)[22] is a great way to silence your inner critic. It is a psychotherapy approach that focuses on the connection between thoughts, feelings, and actions, and it offers strategies to change those ways of thinking, feeling, and acting from negative to positive. Here are some ways to implement CBT in your daily life:

Step 1. Initiate a Thought Journal: I've already mentioned the benefits of journaling, and here is another benefit. By keeping a daily record of your thoughts, especially those that feel particularly intense or recurring, you'll have a tangible record of your mental landscape over time, making patterns easier to spot.

Analyze the Situations: If you have repetitive thoughts like *I'm not good enough* or *I'm not as good as they think I am*, if possible, write down the situation, event, or even the person connected with the situation that initiated these thoughts. Was it a comment from a colleague? A mistake you made? An unexpected event? By understanding the situations that breed negativity, you can be better prepared or even avoid them in the future.

Look for Triggers: Feelings can also ignite negative thoughts. Analyze when you're more self-critical. Is it when you're tired or overwhelmed? By recognizing what might trigger your negative feelings, you may be able to reason with that inner voice and not accept that negative self-talk as truthful.

Look for Patterns: As you compile more entries in your thought journal, take time each week to review and identify recurring themes or triggers. Are there specific times of day when you're more negative? Or perhaps there are certain people or environments that frequently spark a spiral of negative thinking?

Step 2. Challenge the Thoughts: Once you identify a pattern, question it. Is the negative thought based on facts or assumptions? Often, we accept our thoughts as truths without challenging them. By interrogating these thoughts, we can discern between what's a genuine concern and what's merely a product of our inner critic. And writing those thoughts helps create some distance, which may make it easier to assess the truthfulness of them. As you read your negative thought(s), ask yourself these questions:

- Is this thought based on emotion or facts?

- What evidence is there that this thought is accurate?

- What evidence is there that this thought isn't accurate?

- How could I test this belief?

- What's the worst that could happen? How could I respond if the worst happens?

- What other ways could this information be interpreted?

- Is this really a black-and-white situation or are there shades of gray here?

Step 3. Reframe and Replace: Now, consciously counter these negative thoughts with more realistic and positive affirmations. Instead of "I can't do this," tell yourself, "I'll give it my best shot."

Positive affirmations play a pivotal role in this restructuring. These are short, powerful statements that help overcome self-sabotaging thoughts. Some examples include:

"I believe in myself."
"I am able, smart and capable, and enough."
"Every challenge I face is an opportunity to grow."

But remember, for affirmations to be effective, they should resonate with you. Craft ones that feel genuine and align with your goals.

Continuously practicing positive self-talk is paramount. The more you repeat affirmations and challenge negative thoughts, the stronger your new, positive neural pathways become. It's akin to building muscle memory: with time and practice, positive self-talk becomes a reflex.

Yet despite our best efforts, there will be times when negativity seeps in. Remember, the brain is an ever-evolving organ. Negative patterns that have taken years to establish won't dissipate overnight. Each day, each positive affirmation, and each act of self-kindness takes you a step closer to a mental space where optimism reigns supreme. **By recognizing, challenging, and reframing, you're not only silencing the inner critic but also empowering your true self.** And with time this true self becomes the dominant voice, guiding you with confidence, compassion, and clarity. Each effort made toward this end is a step closer to self-empowerment and genuine self-acceptance.

Note: While following the self-help CBT steps I've suggested can be effective for many, it is not meant to be a replacement for professional therapy. If you're dealing with serious issues, please consult a mental health professional.

Mindfulness Meditation: This practice centers the mind and breath on the present moment without judgment. It involves trying to clear your mind by focusing on being in the moment and breathing. And when your mind wanders—which it will—recognize it and, without any negativity, simply acknowledge it and direct it back to your breath.

The "Best Friend" Technique: When confronted with a barrage of self-deprecating thoughts, ask yourself, "Would I say this to my best friend?" Most often, we're harder on ourselves than we would be on someone we care about. By distancing yourself and examining your thoughts from a third-person perspective, it becomes easier to identify the harshness in them.

Set Boundaries with External Negativity: Often, negative self-talk is fueled by external factors, like a critical peer or unrealistic societal standards from social media. If you recognize your trigger is an external source that intensifies your internal critic, please limit exposure to it. This might mean setting boundaries with a negative friend or family member, cutting down on social media usage, or avoiding certain triggering environments.

Practice Gratitude: One of the easiest ways to shift your mindset from negative to positive is to simply feel grateful for all the good things in your life. By consistently recognizing and acknowledging things in a positive light, you will actually rewire your brain to focus on the positives. When we feel genuine thankfulness, our attention moves from negativity to positivity. And that shift can have profound effects on our state of mind. Writing in a daily gratitude journal or incorporating daily "wins" into dinner conversations with your family will impact your outlook and move you toward a feeling of abundance resulting in overall happiness. By simply acknowledging all the things in your life you have to be grateful for (even the smallest things count), you will begin to see things in a new and positive light.

One of my clients, whom we'll call Holly, was a successful high achiever who impressed everyone she crossed paths with. However, internally, Holly was grappling with anxiety, impostor syndrome, and insomnia. When she finally opened up to me, she admitted that she knew her current way of living wasn't working, but she didn't know what to do. Her inner turmoil was taking its toll, and she was finally ready to take action . . . she just needed direction.

Her journey began with meditation and Mindfulness practices. Each day, Holly devoted time to pausing, breathing, and resetting her busy mind through moments of mindfulness and focused meditation.

CBT also played an important part of her transformation. Holly learned to identify and analyze negative thought patterns that played on an internal loop and fueled her feelings of anxiety and impostor syndrome. She began to replace the irrational thoughts with empowering ones, which helped to rewire her brain and improve her self-confidence.

She also turned her attention to her physical health by exercising and eating healthy foods, which greatly improved her mental health. Encouraged by each improvement, Holly recognized the importance of positive self-talk and reframed her inner dialogue to one that she could be proud of.

When combined, these various self-help techniques resulted in Holly feeling lighter and happier. Her story isn't unique, however, as I've seen this transformation in so many who have embraced the work and reaped the rewards. And I know that you, too, can find the peace and well-being you're searching for by following similar steps. Your life is worth the effort.

SHARPENING THOSE "DULL EDGES"

Those "dull edges" we talked about involve the battlefield of the mind, so the best way to sharpen your sword is a five-step self-affirmation process. These steps should be taken regularly. Remember the analogy of the frog in the boiling pot of water? The same rules apply. You don't want to be in the throes of insecurity and self-sabotage before you take action.

Step 1. Be Self-Aware

Acknowledge your strengths first. This is the first step to the self-affirmation process before proceeding with any changes. Write down your accomplishments, skills, and traits that have contributed to your past successes—this will help you get a clearer picture of your potential.

Step 2. Identify Areas of Growth

Through self-reflection, identify areas where you feel less confident or where you could improve. These could be skills, character traits, or even aspects of personal wellness like emotional health or fitness. Remember to approach this with kindness and understanding—these are not failures but opportunities for growth.

Step 3. Create Positive Affirmations

Turn your identified areas of improvement into positive affirmations. For example, if you struggle with public speaking, an affirmation might be: "I am confident and articulate in expressing my thoughts." Try to phrase your affirmations in the present tense and in positive terms so that they embody what you aim to become.

Step 4. Practice Daily

Consistency is key with most things in life, and it's essential in changing your outlook. By incorporating positive affirmations into your daily routine, you'll be able to rewire your brain and turn your negative thoughts into positive beliefs. Write down your affirmations, read them often, and begin saying them aloud in front of the mirror regularly.

Step 5. Evaluate and Adjust

Periodically review and assess how effective the affirmations and this process are. Are you making progress toward your goal? Are you feeling more confident? If the answer is not a resounding yes, don't get discouraged. Adjust the affirmations or your method of practicing, taking note of what feels truly affirming for you. Reflect on your experiences and adapt your techniques to suit your evolving needs and experiences.

Remember that change takes time and practice, so be patient with yourself throughout this process. Even the smallest progress is a step in the right direction.

THE PERILS OF PEOPLE-PLEASING AND THE POWER TO PUSH PAST

High-achieving women have a distinct strength, a burning drive that propels them forward. Yet for many, the prospect of upsetting someone or being the source of disappointment becomes their shortcoming. The persistent desire to be liked and avoid conflict, often deeply ingrained, can be a heavy weight to bear.

Being a people pleaser often stems from a firmly established fear of displeasing others. The mere idea of someone being mad or upset with you feels like a personal failure. While pleasing people can be rooted in kindness, it becomes problematic when done at the expense of your own needs and well-being. It's a trait shaped by past experiences and, perhaps, by nature itself. Whether it's a childhood event, societal expectations, or an innate trait, this yearning to make everyone happy can take a toll.

When you bite your tongue, ignore your own feelings, or suppress the urge to stand up for yourself, you're planting seeds of regret. Over time, these unsaid words and unmet needs erode self-confidence and self-love. It's like an inner battle where you get mad at yourself for not setting boundaries, thus letting someone exploit your good nature.

RECOGNIZING TRIGGERS: THE FIRST STEP TO EMPOWERMENT

Research has shown that recognizing our feelings and triggers is a key step in empowerment. When you feel that familiar tug of anxiety or fear, especially when someone asks more of you than you're prepared to give, stop and acknowledge it. It's a trigger, and it's okay to feel it.

A study published in the *Journal of Social and Personal Relationships*[23] found that individuals who acknowledged their feelings felt more in control and were less likely to react impulsively. So, when that client or colleague asks for an extra favor, or when your boss piles on another task, recognize your feelings. By doing so, you're halfway there.

STRATEGIES FOR NAVIGATING TRIGGERS

Every situation demands a unique approach, but you having a few prepared statements can be a lifesaver. Here are a couple that may help you:

For Clients: "I genuinely want to make that happen for you. Let me consult with the team, and I'll get back to you shortly." This response allows you to take a breather, think logically, and come up with a solution or counterproposal.

For Bosses or Colleagues: "I understand the importance of this request. Can we discuss how to prioritize this with my current tasks?" It's assertive yet collaborative, showing you're on the same team but need clarity.

Work on coming up with a few "statements" so you have them in your back pocket when needed. I know it sounds strange to prepare this way, but it will help stop you from saying yes when you really want to say no.

In these heated moments, remember that it's natural to feel fear or anxiety. But also remember your power.

HARNESSING POWER POSES

Dr. Amy Cuddy's research on "power poses" has been a game changer for many professionals. In her 2012 TED Talk[24], which has been viewed nearly 70 million times, she explains the impact that nonverbal cues (our body language) can have, not only on others, but also on ourselves. Power poses reduce cortisol and increase testosterone, which helps you exude confidence while elevating your mood and assertiveness levels, even when you're feeling down or insecure. For instance, standing tall with your hands on your hips (think of a superhero) or stretching your arms out wide in a V shape (think of a runner at the finish line) for as little as two minutes can boost your confidence before heading into a challenging situation like a job interview or presentation.

In my experience, Amy Cuddy's power poses have been a real game changer. Despite my usual confidence in addressing large audiences, I encountered unexpected nerves in a new role as a wedding officiant. This was a departure from my typical presentations and talks, where I felt like an expert. The importance of the occasion for the bride and groom made me anxious. However, I found a solution. Retreating to the ladies' room, I struck the Superwoman pose. It was remarkable how quickly this simple act boosted my confidence, helping me step back into the ceremony with renewed poise and assurance.

Think about your challenging encounters and take a moment to write out your feelings. Reflect on what went well and what you'd do differently next time. And don't forget to pat yourself on the back for advocating for your needs.

You're a high achiever, and the world is fortunate to have you. While the desire to make everyone around you happy is admirable, your happiness and well-being matter just as much. With understanding, strategy, and a touch of power posing, you can balance your innate kindness with the assertiveness you deserve.

NAVIGATING DISPLEASURE: THE PATH TO INNER STRENGTH FOR HIGH ACHIEVERS

As much as we'd all love to please everyone, the truth is that it's never going to happen. Navigating that displeasure successfully takes practice, especially when our internal alarms are going off.

Mind's Echo: The thoughts that surface often revolve around self-doubt. "Did I do something wrong?" "Will they dislike me now?" "I should've done things differently." These are common refrains. You might also find your mind constantly replaying conversations or incidents, hunting for signs or moments where things might have gone amiss.

The Body's Alarm: For many, the sensation begins as a tightening in the chest or stomach. A cold rush might surge through your extremities, or your heart rate might quicken. There's a general feeling of unease often accompanied by shallow breathing or an unsettling feeling in the pit of the stomach.

Recognizing these sensations is paramount. The moment you start to sense them is when you're most vulnerable to making hasty decisions or reacting impulsively in an effort to immediately remedy the situation and avoid conflict.

TECHNIQUES FOR BUILDING TOLERANCE: FROM SENSING TO RESPONDING

1. Grounding Techniques: When you recognize those early signs of anxiety, employ grounding techniques to keep you present. This can be as simple as deep breathing, tapping your fingers rhythmically, or feeling the texture of a nearby object.

2. Fact-Check Your Thoughts: Challenge the immediate negative narratives that spring up. For instance, when the thought *They must be so mad at me* crosses your mind, counter it with *I don't have enough evidence of that yet* or *It's possible they're dealing with their own issues.*

3. Delay the Response: When in doubt, buy time. Instead of instantly seeking to appease or remedy, give yourself permission to say, "I need some time to think about this" or "Let me get back to you." This provides a window to process logically.

4. Practice Assertive Communication: Voicing your feelings and boundaries is crucial. Remember, being assertive doesn't mean being aggressive. It's about expressing your needs clearly and respectfully.

5. Reflect and Reevaluate: Take a moment to reflect on the situation. Or talk to a trusted friend or therapist. What triggered your feelings? How did you respond? Over time, these reflections or another perspective can offer insights into patterns and offer ways to break free from the reflexive need to please.

EMBRACING AUTHENTICITY

The path of a high achiever isn't devoid of challenges, but each challenge offers an opportunity for growth. By recognizing the signs of impending conflict and employing strategies to manage them, you can evolve from being a perpetual people pleaser to an empowered individual who stands firm in authenticity. Remember, it's not about never upsetting anyone, it's about staying true to yourself while navigating the many relationships and responsibilities in your life.

REFLECTION

- Can you recall a recent incident where you felt the immediate physical sensations of displeasure or potential conflict? Where in your body did you feel it most intensely?

- Think of the last time you believed someone was upset with you. What were the dominant thoughts that ran through your mind?

- Have you tried any grounding techniques in the past? Which ones felt most effective, and why?

- Reflect on a past situation where your initial perception was that someone was displeased with you. Was that perception accurate? Could there have been other factors at play?

- Think of a time when you successfully communicated your needs or boundaries. How did it feel afterward?

- Was there ever a situation where you wish you had taken more time before responding? How do you think delaying your response might have changed the outcome?

- How do you envision your journey from people-pleasing to assertive communication in the next year? Are there specific steps or milestones you hope to achieve?

- Do you currently have a support system, whether friends, family, or professionals, where you can discuss your feelings and challenges related to people-pleasing? If not, how might you begin to build that network?

- Think about future situations that might involve conflict or displeasure. How will you prepare yourself for them? Are there steps you can take to feel more confident? What affirmations can you tell yourself to help change your mindset?

CHAPTER 4:
FROM CONFUSION TO CLARITY

We do not see things as they are, we see them as we are.
–Anaïs Nin

High-achieving women stride powerfully through life, often achieving goals many might find unattainable. Their journeys, charged with ambition and determination, are rarely linear. It's amid this intricate web of aspirations that confusion can cloud the path, especially when pivotal decisions loom. Why do strong, capable women sometimes grapple with decision-making, and how can they transition from confusion to clarity?

WHY CAN CLARITY PLAY HIDE-AND-SEEK WITH HIGH ACHIEVERS?

The Perfectionist's Paradox: It may be contradictory, but being a perfectionist may be what is holding many high-achieving women back from actually achieving more. That driving force to work tirelessly to deliver perfect results can sometimes lead to a fear of failure. And it's that fear that prevents them from taking a step forward in case it's an imperfect step. A fear of failure can result in analysis paralysis, where they overthink their next move and decide against any move in case it's the wrong one. Often, when a decision needs to be made, there may not be one right decision. That fuzzy concept can contribute to emotional exhaustion and overwhelming confusion.

The Weight of Expectations: Lofty aspirations are a double-edged sword. One side gleams with self-set goals, and the other side is weighed down by external pressures. Confusion can be the byproduct of balancing expectations of yourself with others.

The Shadows of Past Failures: An intense aversion to failure is a frequent companion of high achievers. Humans are not just logical beings, they're emotional ones. A past failure isn't just remembered in the context of what went wrong and why but also in terms of how it felt. The embarrassment, disappointment, or shame experienced during past failures can create a visceral reaction, making high-achieving women wary of experiencing those emotions again.

The Over-Commitment Maze: Relentless busyness, a trap many high achievers find themselves in, is especially tricky because being constantly busy has a ripple effect. Our brains, although amazing, have their limit to cognitive resources. We now know that constant multitasking and the pressure to manage a plethora of tasks can lead to cognitive overload. When the brain is overwhelmed, decision-making processes are compromised, leading to indecision or poor choices.

Continual busyness leaves little room for reflection. Without regular self-reflection, it's difficult to gain clarity about one's desires, priorities, and the long-term implications of decisions.

Of course, there is always the fear you might miss something. The feeling of wanting to seize every opportunity can lead to a fear of missing out (FOMO). This FOMO mindset can result in a failure to say no when necessary, further amplifying the cycle of busyness and making decisions based on external pressures rather than internal alignment.

And this is a bit scary—constant busyness might diminish one's emotional intelligence (EI), which is the ability to recognize and control your emotions, as well as understand and deal with the emotions of others.

This concept of EI was developed by psychologists Peter Salovey and John Mayer and popularized by Daniel Goleman in the 1990s. According to Harvard Business School, EI "is one of the most sought-after interpersonal skills in the workplace. In fact, 71 percent of employers value emotional intelligence more than technical skills when evaluating candidates."[25]

Those with high EI are able to remain calm under pressure, resolve conflicts, and make thoughtful decisions. And having high EI extends to all areas of your life, not just at work. Think of being able to better manage toddler temper tantrums and family strife.

Solitary Struggles: High achievers often hesitate to seek help, viewing it as an admittance of inadequacy. In their quest to uphold the image of the ever-capable achiever, they unintentionally close doors to potential solutions and insights.

Navigating the Conscious and Unconscious: Our conscious thoughts, deliberate and intentional, guide our immediate decisions. Simultaneously, our unconscious mind, operating behind the scenes, often influences these decisions based on past experiences, biases, and deep-seated fears. Recognizing and reconciling this interplay is fundamental for clarity. For instance, a decision might seem logical when analyzed consciously, but unconscious fears may deter its execution.

REFLECTING ON MY OWN INDECISION

I experienced the power of the unconscious firsthand. Many years ago I was working for a company and desperately wanted to move to an organization that was more aligned with who I was. My values were being compromised, especially when I recognized I was not only working for a misogynist but was also working with misogynists who felt compelled to comment on female clients' physical appearances. I got an offer to work for a company I respect. Instead of jumping at the opportunity and celebrating, I was weighed down as layers of internal turmoil emerged. Consciously, I had logical reasons not to move: surface-level hesitations, like a binding non-compete clause. But somehow, those reasons veiled deeper fears and doubts. Recognizing this duality, the conscious and unconscious interplay, was transformative. I could face the fears head-on. It was through my own experience, as well as my experience in helping my clients with indecision and confusion, that I developed the following process to move from confusion to clarity

FINDING CLARITY: STEPS OUT OF THE MAZE

The Power of Naming Emotions

Dr. Dan Siegel, a clinical professor of psychiatry at the UCLA School of Medicine and the founding codirector of the Mindful Awareness Research Center at UCLA said, "When we can name it, we can tame it."[26] Dr. Siegel's profound insight into the human psyche underscores the significance of recognizing and naming our emotions. By acknowledging how we feel, we empower ourselves to process, manage, and ultimately harness those feelings to our advantage.

Here's a deeper exploration of this concept:

Awareness Through Language: Language gives shape to our emotional world. When we put a label on what we're feeling, we create a cognitive framework that can help process the emotion. For instance, distinguishing between being anxious and being frustrated paves the way for tailored coping mechanisms for each emotion.

The Biology of Naming: The very act of naming an emotion that we're feeling can have a calming effect on our brain. By engaging our prefrontal cortex, which is the area that regulates our thoughts and actions, we reduce the activity in our amygdala, which is the area responsible for feelings of fight or flight. Thus, the very easy exercise of recognizing and labeling our emotion can reduce the intensity of that feeling.

Emotion as Information: Emotions serve as data. For instance, fear might indicate a potential threat, while excitement can signal a beneficial opportunity. By acknowledging emotions and dissecting them, we can glean insights that guide our decision-making process.

Defusing Emotional Charges: Let's say you're feeling overwhelmed but can't pin down why. By sifting through your emotions and identifying that it's, say, anxiety stemming from uncertainty about a future event, you're already on a clearer path. Identifying the emotion often reduces its grip on you, as it now feels more manageable and less like an undefined, looming cloud.

The Emotional Compass: Paying attention to your emotions and what sparks a particular feeling can act like a compass pointing toward what you're aligned with and away from what causes friction.

Empathy and Connection: Naming our emotions isn't just beneficial for personal understanding, it's also foundational for interpersonal relationships. Sharing how you feel creates an emotional bridge, fostering understanding and connection with others. When you articulate your feelings, it also gives others the permission to do the same, promoting mutual understanding.

The Healing Power of Journaling for Insight

Externalizing the Internal: The sheer act of translating thoughts into words gives form to the abstract. It's like holding up a mirror to your mind, allowing you to see your thoughts more objectively. By giving voice to your innermost feelings, you're separating them from yourself, making them easier to analyze and understand.

Identifying Patterns: Over time, as you leaf back through your entries, patterns might emerge. Maybe you notice that certain events, people, or situations trigger specific emotions or responses. Recognizing these patterns can offer valuable insights into how your mind works and what influences your mood and decisions.

Organizing Chaos: Our minds can be a maze of thoughts, some interconnected, some disjointed. Journaling helps untangle this web. As you write, you're effectively streamlining your thoughts, prioritizing them, and discerning which are crucial and which can be let go.

Safe Space for Expression: A journal is a nonjudgmental space. It doesn't interrupt, argue, or criticize. It simply listens. For individuals who might not feel comfortable sharing their deepest fears, hopes, or feelings with others, personal writing offers a confidential sanctuary.

Written Words Have Power: The very act of writing down problems can clear the mind of confusion, often allowing solutions to emerge. Similarly, with thoughts, seeing affirmations or achievements on paper can strengthen your resolve and confidence in a way that mere thoughts can't.

Emotional Release: For many, this act can be cathartic. By pouring out worries, frustrations, or sadness onto paper, you might feel a weight lifted off your shoulders. It's akin to having a conversation with a trusted confidant.

Mindfulness and Awareness: Journaling requires you to be present and focus on the task at hand. Writing forces you to slow down, compose your thoughts, and reflect, which can result in a meditative-like calm. Over time, regular journaling also forges an awareness of your emotions and triggers.

Decoding Avoidance Patterns in Decision-Making

Avoidance is a crafty, subtle, often camouflaged defense mechanism that we all resort to at various moments in our life. Avoidance usually comes from fearing the unknown. But when it comes to making decisions, particularly pivotal ones, avoidance can become a significant roadblock. Here's a closer examination of why understanding our avoidance patterns is crucial and how you can navigate around them:

The Camouflage of Busyness: One common manifestation of avoidance is busyness. It's easy to bury oneself in work, household chores, or even social obligations to sidestep a looming decision. By understanding that busyness can be a cloak for avoidance, you're one step closer to confronting the real issue.

Mental Loops and Ruminations: Another sign of avoidance is getting trapped in a loop of overthinking without arriving at a concrete decision. While reflection is valuable, incessant rumination without direction can be a subtle way our minds delay confronting a decision.

Distraction as a Defense: Our minds are ingenious at creating distractions. Maybe you suddenly have an urge to reorganize your wardrobe or delve into a new hobby when there's a pressing decision on the horizon. Recognizing these impulses as possible avoidance strategies is key.

Sometimes the signs are physical. A nagging headache, upset stomach, or just a general sense of unease can all be indicators you're wrestling with avoidance. Likewise, you might feel anxious or irritable when you're avoiding making a decision. Paying attention to your body and mind can give you valuable insights into patterns of avoidance.

To truly understand and tackle avoidance, one must be brave enough to delve deep. Why are you avoiding the decision? Is it fear of failure? Or perhaps fear of success? Maybe it's the weight of others' expectations or the terror of charting unknown territory. Asking why repeatedly, peeling back the layers, can help unearth the underlying reason.

By reflecting on past decisions and identifying moments where avoidance came into play, you can discern patterns.

Maybe you always avoid decisions linked to finances, or perhaps choices that might lead to confrontation. Recognizing these patterns can equip you to tackle future decisions head-on.

Understanding your avoidance patterns isn't about self-blame, it's about self-awareness. Approach the realization with compassion, understanding that avoidance is a natural, human response to discomfort or fear.

Once you've pinpointed your avoidance triggers and patterns, it's about seeking strategies to counter them. Maybe it's breaking the decision into smaller steps, seeking counsel, or setting specific timelines.

In essence, unraveling the enigma of avoidance is like assembling a jigsaw puzzle. Each piece, each insight, brings clarity. And with clarity comes the empowerment to make decisions with confidence and conviction. Remember, recognizing the pattern is half the battle won. The rest is about arming yourself with the right strategies and a dollop of self-compassion.

Insight Brings Clarity: Before one of my coaching clients, Tess, was to begin her own business, she met with me to help hone focus on her path forward. As she began self-reflection, she was surprised to uncover long-buried emotions bubbling to the surface. She wasn't accustomed to such vulnerability, but she soon realized that in order to gain the clarity she sought, she first needed to work through this in a way that resonated with her. We worked together to discover that she was an external processor, so I encouraged her to write out and talk about her emotions, desires, and fears. She was soon able to clearly see her core values, her priorities, and her purpose.

You see, whether you're an internal processor (a thinker) or an external one (a talker and writer), there's no one-size-fits-all approach. It's all about understanding and embracing your unique process and tailoring your approach to your own processing style.

Consulting and Counseling: Remember, you don't have to navigate complex decisions in isolation. Seeking external input can be incredibly beneficial. Engaging with a trusted friend, family member, or a professional can introduce fresh perspectives or even highlight considerations you hadn't thought of. However, a word of caution: While it's helpful to gather varied viewpoints, don't let them overshadow your own instincts and values. **The aim is to use external advice as a guide, not as a substitute for your own judgment. After all, you're the best expert on your own life and aspirations.**

Sit with Your Decision: Once you've reached a decision, resist the urge to immediately spring into action. Instead, let it marinate in your mind for a while. Give yourself the space to reflect, to feel its weight, its implications. Does it resonate with your inner self? Can you see it fitting seamlessly into the broader picture of your goals and aspirations? Taking this pause ensures you're moving forward with intention and confidence.

Trust Yourself: In the end, you need to be able to truly trust in yourself. Everyone has a unique path that has led them to where they are now. Embrace your journey and recognize that the decisions you made along the way were instrumental in shaping you in some way. Self-reflection can help you own them and learn from them.

We all have moments of confusion, but as high-achieving women, the journey from confusion to clarity isn't just about reaching a destination, it's about understanding the intricacies of one's mind and heart. With introspection, patience, and courage, clarity isn't just attainable, it's inevitable.

REFLECTION

This exercise will help you gain clarity by reflecting on the insights we've discussed. You'll need a quiet space and paper and pen.

Step 1: Name Your Emotions

Objective: Understand the emotions underlying your confusion.

Close your eyes and take a few deep breaths to calm and center yourself. Then ask yourself, "What am I feeling right now?"

Jot down every emotion that surfaces—without judgment.

Step 2: Journaling for Insights

Objective: Identify patterns, concerns, and reflections tied to your confusion.

Begin writing about a situation or decision that is causing confusion.

As you write, let your thoughts flow freely. Don't overthink or judge them.

Do you see any themes or patterns in your thoughts?

Step 3: Affirmation and Validation

Objective: Strengthen your self-confidence.

On a new page, list down five achievements you're proud of.

Write five positive affirmations about yourself. (Example: "I am capable of making informed decisions.")

Whenever doubt creeps in, revisit these affirmations.

Step 4: Unearth Avoidance Patterns

Objective: Identify how you deal with avoidance.

Reflect on any recent activities or tasks you've taken up unexpectedly. Are any of them out of character or not pressing?

Are these activities a means of diverting your mind from the issue at hand? Do you notice any triggers or patterns of avoidance?

Step 5: The Deep Dive

Objective: Delve into the reasons behind your confusion.

Ask yourself, "Why am I feeling this way?" Write down your answer.

Continue the chain by asking *why* to your previous response. For instance, if your answer was "I'm afraid of making the wrong choice," ask "Why am I afraid of making the wrong choice?"

Continue this until you feel you've reached the root cause. This process will help in unearthing deeper emotions and reasons.

Step 6: External vs. Internal Processing

Objective: Understand your processing mechanism.

Reflect on past decisions. Did discussing them with someone help you gain clarity? Or did introspection lead to a solution?

Identify whether you lean more toward external or internal processing.

Use this insight for future decision-making processes. If you're an external processor, consider discussing issues with a trusted friend. If internal, set aside quiet time for reflection.

After completing this exercise, give yourself a moment. Remember, clarity often comes in waves, and it's beneficial to revisit these steps whenever you find yourself in a haze of uncertainty. Celebrate each step toward understanding yourself better!

CHAPTER 5:
NAVIGATING PERSONALITIES AND BUILDING STRONGER BONDS

We are more alike, my friends, than we are unalike.
–Maya Angelou

High achievers can struggle with interpersonal communication for a number of reasons. We become too busy to pause and manage people and relationships because the task is all we can focus on or even see. But these continuous efforts to excel can cause a significant imbalance in our lives, resulting in the neglect of relationships. And at the end of the day, good business comes down to good relationships, and not just with our clients, but with our peers, our team members, and our supervisors too.

Ultimately, we have a critical question to answer about ourselves: What do we do when the need to achieve is bigger than our need to connect?

First, it's important to acknowledge that your drive to achieve is not the issue at hand. As I've explained, being a high achiever has likely contributed to your success thus far, and you may be content with continually striving for the next milestone. However, there may come a time when the price you pay for your achievements outweighs the benefits.

This is typically the case when we struggle to get along with others. Relationships become the collateral damage of our relentless pursuit of goals. When we prioritize accomplishments over connections, we risk alienating those who matter most to us. Achieving a balance between ambition and interpersonal relationships is crucial. After all, true success is not measured by the number of accolades we accumulate but by the bonds we nurture and the positive impact we leave on others. **It's essential to remember that while milestones are important, the journey and the people we share them with are equally, if not more, valuable.**

UNLOCKING THE POWER OF RELATIONSHIPS

In the rapid-paced journey of high-achieving women, the significance of interpersonal relationships often becomes the unsung hero. While accolades and milestones are public markers of success, the tapestry of relationships we weave silently propels us forward, offering support, insight, and the occasional reality check. Harnessing the full power of these relationships amplifies our trajectory in ways we might not even recognize.

FIVE TIPS TO ELEVATE INTERPERSONAL DYNAMICS

1. Conscious Communication: Be aware that communication goes beyond mere words. Body language matters immensely. Maintain eye contact, smile, and put your phone down when you're interacting with others. Be an active listener; lean in and pay attention when someone is talking to you. Not only does this help you understand what's being said, active listening also respects the other person by validating their point of view.

2. Cultivate Mutual Growth: The most enriching relationships are those where growth is a shared goal. Whether it's a professional relationship or a personal one, look for ways to support each other's development. Check in regularly with those important to you to maintain the relationship.

3. Resolve Conflicts Gracefully: Disagreements are natural. However, approaching them with respect, an open mind, and the intent to understand can turn potential conflicts into moments of deepened connection.

4. Celebrate the Small Moments: While grand achievements are spectacular, it's the small, everyday moments that form the heart of relationships. Acknowledging and celebrating these can enhance the depth and quality of your connections.

5. Set Clear Boundaries: High-achieving women often feel the pressure to be "always on." However, setting clear boundaries—both for ourselves and others—is essential for healthy relationships. It's not just about saying no to what we don't want but about saying yes to what truly aligns with our values and priorities.

The realm of high achievement isn't solitary. Every milestone reached is often a testament to a network of relationships that have offered wisdom, resilience, and encouragement. Harnessing relationships helps garner success. By consciously investing in these relationships, we not only enhance our personal and professional lives but also create a ripple effect, inspiring and uplifting those around us.

NAVIGATING THE DYNAMICS OF PERSONALITIES

As we delve deeper into the intricacies of interpersonal relationships, there's a powerful tool that can significantly enhance our understanding and interactions: the knowledge of personality types. Think of it as having a map in a foreign city. While every individual is unique, understanding personality types can provide us with broad outlines, helping us predict patterns, appreciate differences, and communicate more effectively. It's not about boxing people into categories but about appreciating the diverse ways we all think, feel, and operate. Just as we tailor our approach when communicating with someone from a different cultural background, understanding personality types offers us a lens to better perceive and respond to the varied ways people express themselves. Let's dive in and uncover how harnessing the power of personality types can be an asset in enhancing and improving our relationships.

IT'S NOT PERSONAL—IT'S PERSONALITY

Understanding personality preferences isn't just an academic endeavor, it's a profound journey into the depths of who we are, how we interact with others, and, most importantly, how we can thrive while we connect with a diverse group of people.

In human interactions, we occasionally encounter individuals who profoundly resonate with our very essence. I had such an experience years ago when I was starting my business. I was at a large work conference and met Rachel. She immediately stood out, not just for her distinct style but also for her commanding presence. When we struck up a conversation, it was like verbal Ping-Pong—ideas flew back and forth, and before I knew it, I wanted her on my team. And lucky for me, she agreed!

Our collaboration began as seamlessly as our first meeting; however, over time, friction arose. Interestingly, what initially drew us together—our strong convictions and problem-solving skills—soon brought challenges we hadn't anticipated.

In pursuit of resolution and harmony, we sought guidance from a coach. Through these sessions, a realization dawned on me: Often, I gravitated toward individuals who mirrored aspects of my personality. This attraction, while offering comfort in familiarity, also posed challenges, particularly when it came to mutual accommodation. We learned that by understanding and accepting our shared traits, we could forge a strong partnership through logic-driven communication.

This experience was the catalyst for my exploration of various personality types, and for the past two decades, I've been incorporating this knowledge into my practice to help countless clients.

Understanding the four core personalities isn't just about listening to what people say but also observing how they say it. Body language, tone of voice, and other nonverbal cues can offer deep insights into these personality archetypes. Let's delve deeper.

THE FOUR CORE PERSONALITY TYPES

1. THE DYNAMIC DRIVER

Key Traits:

Assertiveness, Competitiveness, Ambition, Tenacity, Self-Assuredness

Key Strengths:

Quick decision-making
Ability to motivate others
Clear vision and goal orientation

Body Language and Tone:

Posture—Stands tall and confident; makes direct eye contact.
Tone—Firm and self-assured; tends to speak with authority and certainty.
Gestures—Often uses hands to make a point.

Recognition Tip:

They're usually the ones leading a discussion or who seem to naturally take charge and make decisions.

2. THE ANALYTICAL THINKER

Key Traits:

Detail-Oriented, Structured, Logical, Systematic, Observant

Key Strengths:

Can stay focused for a long period of time
High precision and accuracy in tasks
Dependability and consistency

Body Language and Tone:

Posture—Might lean forward when explaining or analyzing; maintains steady eye contact.
Tone—Measured and precise.
Gestures—Draws details in the air with fingers.

Recognition Tip:

They are usually the ones asking detailed questions and pausing before answering.

3. THE EMPATHETIC NURTURER

Key Traits:

Compassionate, Intuitive, Patient, Supportive

Key Strengths:

Strong interpersonal skills
Ability to defuse tense situations
Genuine care and concern for others

Body Language and Tone:

Posture—Tends to lean in, showing genuine interest; maintains warm and welcoming eye contact.
Tone—Positive and gentle.
Gestures—Nods during listening and might touch their heart to convey emotion.

Recognition Tip:

They're the ones actively listening to others and using positive language.

4. THE ENTHUSIASTIC INNOVATOR

Key Traits:

Charisma, Spontaneity, Persuasiveness, Optimism, Visionary

Key Strengths:

Creative thinking
Ability to inspire and rally people
Adaptability to changing circumstances

Body Language and Tone:

Posture—Moves with energy and might change positions frequently; animated facial expressions.

Tone—Expressive and enthusiastic; varies pitch and volume to keep listeners engaged.

Gestures—Big hand movements to paint ideas and show excitement.

Recognition Tip:

They're the ones who are the center of attention, with stories to tell.

INTROVERSION/EXTROVERSION

Introversion and extraversion, two terms you might've heard before, are all about where we get our energy. Think of extroverts as those friends who are energized by bustling parties, group chats, and meeting new people. They thrive in lively settings and love sharing their stories. On the flip side, introverts are the friends who find joy in cozy evenings with a book or deep one-on-one chats over coffee. They recharge in quieter environments. Now, when we talk about our Four Cornerstones of Personality, you might find the Dynamic Driver and the Enthusiastic Innovator often dancing in the extrovert's corner. Meanwhile, the Analytical Thinker and the Empathetic Nurturer might be chilling with the introvert crowd. But here's the fun twist! Many of us are a blend of both, called ambiverts! That's right; a lot of us find energy in both social settings and alone time. Ambiverts may love a party, but they won't be the last to leave. And just to clear the air, no style is "better" than the other. Whether you're an introvert, extrovert, or somewhere in between, you bring your own kind of magic to the party!

And people have qualities from all four types. This is the paradox of personality—we can be more than one type and are often a blend. Recognizing these types isn't about pigeonholing people but about understanding and appreciating their prominent type with their inherent strengths and styles of communication. It provides a foundation for enhanced empathy, collaboration, and mutual respect.

THE PITFALLS OF EACH PERSONALITY TYPE

Carl Jung, the pioneering Swiss psychiatrist and psychoanalyst, postulated that our strengths, when overemphasized or overused, can manifest as weaknesses.[27] This profound insight underscores the delicate equilibrium of our psyche. For Jung, every trait exists on a spectrum, and the magnification of any one characteristic can lead to imbalances in personality, ultimately becoming counterproductive. To him, the very qualities that drive us to achieve greatness can also become our weakness if unchecked. No one personality type is better than another—they all have their advantages and their challenges. Let's look at some of the pitfalls for each personality type:

1. THE DYNAMIC DRIVER

Pitfalls:

Impulsive, Domineering, Intolerant

Why these pitfalls? Their intrinsic need for achievement and progress often pushes them to constantly be on the move. While this ambition is admirable, it can sometimes lead to overlooking details, not allowing space for others, or burnout.

2. THE ANALYTICAL THINKER

Pitfalls:

Resistant to Change, Reluctant to Trust, Detached

Why these pitfalls? Their nature to deeply process and (over) analyze can sometimes prevent them from taking swift actions or adapting to dynamic situations.

3. THE EMPATHETIC NURTURER

Pitfalls:

Avoids Conflict, People-Pleasing, Internalizes Emotions

Why these pitfalls? Their intrinsic desire to maintain peace and provide support can sometimes blur lines, causing them to prioritize others' needs over their own or avoid necessary confrontations.

4. THE ENTHUSIASTIC INNOVATOR

Pitfalls:

Overly Optimistic, Lack of Follow-Through, Impatient

Why these pitfalls? Their passion for innovation and excitement about possibilities can sometimes lead them away from the methodical and consistent processes required for realization.

So, you see, each personality type comes with strengths and challenges. Recognition and understanding are key for personal growth and improved relationships, both at work and personally. After all, knowing how to adapt to and work with the different personalities in our lives will only strengthen each interaction we have with them and alleviate additional stress.

ADAPTING TO EACH PERSONALITY

1. THE DYNAMIC DRIVER

Dynamic Drivers are goal-oriented, so focus on results. Start conversations by highlighting objectives and potential outcomes. They want to understand the end game or the outcome before investing time. Instead of saying, "I think we should consider this marketing strategy," say "Implementing this strategy can increase our sales by 20 percent." They appreciate clarity and succinctness, so get to the point quickly. They prefer straightforwardness over ambiguity or roundabout conversations.

2. THE ANALYTICAL THINKER

Analytical Thinkers are focused on logical reasoning and facts, so be able to back up your points with data and present your case in an organized manner. Instead of saying, "It feels like this would be the best choice," say "Based on our recent sales figures and the following reasons, this is the most viable option moving forward." They may need a moment to process information because they prefer to think things through before giving a response.

3. THE EMPATHETIC NURTURER

Empathetic Nurturers value interpersonal relationships, so ask about their well-being and feelings. Rather than diving straight into facts and figures, take a moment to connect. "Before we get into today's agenda, how are you feeling about the project? I'd love to hear your insight." They flourish with emotional connections, so using language that resonates with them will be beneficial.

4. THE ENTHUSIASTIC INNOVATOR

Enthusiastic Innovators thrive in collaborative and creative environments, so encourage that. "Let's think outside the box and explore some unconventional solutions." And remember to validate their passion by asking for a walkthrough of their ideas before making a judgment.

PERSONALITY CHANGES

A significant point to underscore is the fluid nature of personality. As proposed by Carl Jung, our personalities aren't static. People can wear different personas based on the situation. For instance, the same individual might adopt a different personality at work compared to how they behave at home or with friends.

Jung's work highlighted how these masks could be a reflection of society's expectations. It's as if we don different hats to adapt to different situations. High achievers, being accustomed to diverse settings and expectations, may frequently switch between these personas.

THE OVERWHELM FACTOR

Stress or being overwhelmed can distort these personas. When individuals are overwhelmed, they can become more or less of their "natural" selves. I experienced this firsthand when I was moving from Toronto to Austin.

Just as anxiety about my undelivered belongings peaked, a call informed me of their arrival the next morning. Panic set in. The house, under renovation, wasn't ready. My initial calls to PODS and the contractor were met with barriers, and my assertiveness veered dangerously close to aggression.

When I got in my car to head over to see the contractor to twist his arm, I saw a reflection in the rearview mirror that showed not the determined problem solver I prided myself on being but someone aggressive, argumentative, and rigid. I inhaled deeply, attempting to recalibrate.

Drawing on my logical thinking, I shifted gears. This was a problem—problems have solutions. Instead of bulldozing my way through, what if I tapped into my inherent ability to connect with others? I remembered my gift for seeing the person behind a role, understanding their perspective, and using humor to lighten tense situations.

Returning to my contractor, my approach was different. We laughed about the impeccable timing of my life's events, and together, we brainstormed. The solution? Moving blankets. They'd protect the freshly polished floors, allowing us to transport items upstairs to untouched rooms. He was on board.

Next was the call back to PODS. I made a conscious effort to think of the individual on the other end. Sharing my predicament and understanding their constraints, I was met with empathy. And to my surprise, schedules were shuffled, and my POD was delivered early the next day.

This experience was transformative. It showcased how, in the face of adversity, understanding our strengths and recognizing when they tip into overdrive can be invaluable. Leveraging a diverse set of qualities, rather than over-relying on one, can pave the way to resolutions. In a world where problems are a constant, the real power lies in knowing ourselves and choosing the best version of who we are in any given situation.

Here are some examples of how a personality can shift under stress:

Exaggeration: Someone may amplify their typical traits. An Analytical Thinker might become excessively meticulous to the point of paralysis.

Regression: Some might revert to a more primal version of their personality. A Dynamic Driver might become overly aggressive.

RE-CENTERING THROUGH YOUR STRENGTHS: A GUIDED APPROACH

1. DYNAMIC DRIVER: Challenges can sometimes amplify their tenacity to an overwhelming degree. When feeling off-balance, they can:

Revisit Goals: Reframe and remind oneself of the bigger picture. What are you driving toward? Focus on the primary objectives.

Delegate: You're great at taking charge, so entrust tasks to others if you're spread too thin. This allows you to prioritize and tackle what matters most.

2. ANALYTICAL THINKER: Precision and a love for detail are hallmarks of this type. When things get too chaotic:

Organize: Create lists, use tools, or map out processes. Bringing structure can be incredibly calming.

Research: Dive deep into understanding the problem at hand. Knowledge and a well-laid plan can be your anchor.

3. EMPATHETIC NURTURER: Those with a natural inclination to support and empathize can sometimes feel overwhelmed by others' emotions or circumstances. In such times:

Self-Care: Taking time for yourself can help alleviate stress and center you.

Connect: Talk to someone who uplifts you. Remember, it's okay to seek support when you're usually the one giving it.

4. ENTHUSIASTIC INNOVATOR: The charismatic visionaries have a natural zeal that can sometimes lead to burnout. When that energy feels misdirected:

Creativity: Dive into a new project, sketch, write, or brainstorm. Let your inventive spirit guide you.

Inspiration: Seek stories or endeavors that rekindle your passion. Your innate optimism and visionary outlook can be refueled by looking at the bigger picture.

STEPS TO FINDING COMPOSURE

Acknowledge: Recognize the deviation from your typical self. Understand that it's a momentary lapse, not a permanent shift.

Breathe: Engage in deep, intentional breathing. This centers the mind and body, making way for clearer thought.

Lean On Your Strengths: As highlighted earlier, every personality type has its unique strengths. Reconnect with them.

Reflect: Postulate on the why and the how. Why did this deviation occur? How can your inherent strengths aid in navigating it?

Act: Once you're feeling centered and clear, move forward with intention by leaning on your strengths.

REFLECTION

- Which of the four core personality types do you most closely align with? Why?

- List down five strengths that you believe are inherent to your personality type. Which of these do you find yourself leaning on the most?

- How do you typically respond when stressed? Are there specific triggers that amplify these reactions? Can you identify patterns in your reactions across different stressful scenarios?

- Think of one or two individuals with whom you'd like to foster a better relationship. What is their predominant personality type? How could understanding their strengths and communication style help improve your interactions?

- What are some techniques or methods you could employ to better adapt to these individuals? Are there any practices or habits you'd consider changing or adopting to facilitate smoother interactions?

CHAPTER 6:
GRIT AND RESILIENCE FOR
AN UNYIELDING SPIRIT

I was taught that the way of progress
was neither swift nor easy.
−Marie Curie

Resilience. It's more than a buzzword in today's self-help culture—it's the foundation of true success and lasting achievements, especially for high-achieving women. While society often paints a picture of successful individuals as those who've had a smooth sail to the pinnacle of their professions, it's rarely true. Every success story is built upon resilience—the power to bounce back stronger after setbacks.

While strides have been made, the proverbial glass ceiling hasn't shattered entirely. Women in leadership or high-responsibility roles often encounter subtle biases. Here, resilience is not just helpful, it's imperative.

And if this wasn't enough, we now have the recognition of Tall Poppy Syndrome. Tall Poppy Syndrome refers to the tendency to discredit or undermine individuals who excel in their fields or achieve success, often out of envy or societal discomfort with those who rise above the average. This negative attitude can stifle ambition, curb potential, and discourage individuals from pursuing or celebrating their achievements.

My friend Courtney Clark is a remarkable example of resilience. Not only has she overcome cancer four times and a brain aneurysm, she's also done so with a grace and a fierceness that has strengthened her spirit to soar with purpose. Courtney now shares the life lessons she learned along her inspirational journey with others through her motivational speaking and her informative books. In *The Successful Struggle: Powerful Techniques to Achieve Accelerated Resilience*[28], she focuses on the importance of shifting one's perspective on setbacks to see them as lessons for future growth and success.

RESILIENCE REFINED: A GUIDE FOR THE HIGH-FLYING WOMAN

Acknowledge Your Emotions: Life is a roller coaster of emotions. Especially when you're soaring high, those dips can feel jarring. Whether it's disappointment, frustration, or fear, let yourself feel it. By understanding and acknowledging these emotions, you create the foundation to process and move beyond them.

Embrace Adversity as Opportunity: Think of challenges as the gym for your resilience muscles. Every hurdle is a chance to flex, grow, and emerge stronger. When adversity rears its head, instead of ducking, face it with the confidence that it's another opportunity to evolve.

Set Clear Boundaries: It's wonderful to be driven, but remember: a car running on empty won't go far. Set boundaries to ensure you have moments of rest and recharge. Understand your limits, and don't feel guilty about asserting them. It preserves both your mental health and the quality of your work.

Connect with a Supportive Network: While flying solo has its thrills, having a flock to return to provides comfort. Surround yourself with individuals who lift you higher—mentors, peers, or friends. They offer wisdom, perspective, and sometimes, just the reassuring nod that says, "I get it."

Seek Learning in Every Setback: Courtney Clark's message rings loud and clear. Setbacks are simply setups for comebacks. When faced with challenges, switch your focus from the problem to the lesson it offers. This shift in perspective turns potential discouragement into valuable growth.

Journal: As we've already covered, the very act of writing out our thoughts can be cathartic and provide clarity. Seeing your words on paper can help you process problems, and recording small wins can change your perspective to one of gratitude, which helps with stress.

Revisit Your Values: Whenever doubt casts its shadow, remember what drives you. By staying aligned with your core values, you find the strength to move past temporary hurdles.

Positive Self-Talk: Words have power, especially the ones you tell yourself. In moments of doubt or anxiety, remind yourself of your strength. "I'm a warrior" is not just a phrase, it's an affirmation. In the face of adversity, repeating such affirmations and visualizing yourself as invincible can provide immense comfort and strength.

By integrating these steps into your life, resilience becomes second nature. And remember, for a high-flying woman, the sky isn't the limit, it's just the beginning. **Soar with purpose knowing that resilience is your copilot.** When faced with challenging situations, sometimes it's beneficial to reflect on the generations that came before you. Your lineage is a testament to resilience. My grandmother navigated profound losses—a stillborn child, the passing of her father and brother during the 1917 pandemic, and widowhood. Yet she remained undeterred, working well into her seventies, crafting a life for herself, and living to an inspiring age of 103. These formidable genes flow through your veins, serving as a reservoir of strength to tap in to. My husband's great-grandfather fought in the Civil War. Just visualizing the tenacity required to withstand the challenges of those times can ignite a newfound vigor in my husband. Every time you feel like faltering, remember that your ancestors faced immense challenges, and they not only survived but thrived. Channel their strength, fortitude, and resilience, and remind yourself that it's embedded deep within you.

GRIT

The difference between grit and resilience is subtle yet profound. **While resilience is the capacity to bounce back from setbacks, grit is the sustained passion and perseverance for long-term goals.** It's about stamina and sticking with the journey, day in and day out, rather than a fleeting sprint of enthusiasm. Angela Duckworth, in her pivotal book *Grit: The Power of Passion and Perseverance*[29], unpacks the significance of grit in achieving greatness. She argues that grit, rather than talent, is a better predictor of success. For high-achieving women, understanding and harnessing the power of grit is paramount.

DEVELOPING GRIT: TIPS FOR THE TENACIOUS

Embrace Passion: Find what truly drives you. This isn't a fleeting interest but an inherent passion that gives meaning to your work. When you're aligned with your purpose, perseverance becomes natural.

Cultivate a Growth Mindset: Believe that abilities and intelligence can be developed. It fosters a love for learning and resilience in the face of challenges.

Practice, Practice, Practice: Mastery requires consistent effort. It's the daily discipline, the continual honing of skills that leads to expertise and fuels grit. Develop coping strategies for the inevitable setbacks so you're more confident to deal with them successfully.

Connect with Gritty Individuals: Surround yourself with individuals who exemplify grit. Their stories, guidance, and mere presence can be a constant source of inspiration. I had a birthday party when I invited just my female friends. Several people commented that my friends were all high achievers and many were entrepreneurs. Seeing my friends develop their grit helps me develop mine.

Celebrate Small Wins: Every milestone, no matter how minor, is a testament to your grit. Celebrate these moments; they fuel the journey ahead.

In the realm of high achievement, grit stands tall as a beacon of hope and determination. It's the silent force that propels us forward, ensuring we remain undeterred by challenges and focused on our vision. For every high-achieving woman, nurturing grit is not just an option—it's a necessity.

REFLECTION

- Think of a time you overcame a significant challenge. What did you learn about your resilience?

- Is there someone in your life whose resilience inspired you? What can you learn from their experience?

- How do you currently handle setbacks? How can you shift your perspective to see them as growth opportunities?

- Assess your current level of resilience. What areas do you see as strengths, and where can you grow?

- Think of a time when you needed to rely on your grit. How did it affect the outcome of the situation?

CHAPTER 7:
DISCOVERING PURPOSE—
A JOURNEY TO YOUR TRUE SELF

Purpose. It's a powerful word that resonates with a longing deep within us. But what is purpose? At its core, purpose is our reason for being, the driving force behind our actions, our North Star, and the essence of our existence. It is the underlying essence that fuels passion, dictates objectives, and imparts significance to everyday choices. It is what gives meaning to our life's pursuits and provides us with a sense of direction. Rooted deeply within one's core values and beliefs, purpose serves as the compass guiding life's journey, ensuring alignment with one's truest self and the broader impact they wish to leave on the world. The significance of understanding one's purpose cannot be overstated, especially for high-achieving women who juggle multiple roles and responsibilities.

Purpose gives our life a sense of meaning and direction, which can help prioritize our time and energy. By adhering to what's important to you, you'll be able to live and work with intention. And having a clear understanding of our purpose helps us identify our values and passions, which can ultimately lead to a happier and more fulfilling life. When you have a clear purpose, it becomes the lens through which you view your choices. Every decision, big or small, is seen in the light of this purpose, guiding you toward actions that align with your true intentions and aspirations.

Understanding our larger purpose can also help us form stronger connections. When we clearly understand our purpose, we can better relate to and understand others' unique purposes. This can foster deeper and more meaningful relationships, as we can support and encourage one another in our journeys.

Having a clear purpose also has an impact on health and longevity. The documentary *Live to 100: Secrets of the Blue Zones*[30] examines the correlation between one's purpose and a life well lived. Blue zones refer to specific regions around the world where people live notably longer and healthier lives. Identified through extensive research by Dan Buettner and his team, these zones include locations such as Okinawa (Japan), Sardinia (Italy), Nicoya (Costa Rica), Ikaria (Greece), and Loma Linda (California, USA). One of the striking commonalities among these diverse regions is the emphasis on having a clear sense of purpose. Residents of blue zones often have a well-defined role or reason for getting up in the morning, whether it's community involvement, family, or daily rituals. This ingrained sense of purpose is believed to be a significant contributor to their health, well-being, and longevity, underscoring the profound interplay between mental clarity, purposeful living, and physical health.

PURPOSE VS. GOALS

Purpose is the overarching direction or reason for one's existence, serving as a foundational compass for life's journey. Goals, on the other hand, are specific milestones or targets set along the way to help achieve or manifest that purpose. **While purpose provides the reason behind our actions, goals offer tangible markers to aim for and measure progress.**

As high-achieving women, we are often focused on our goals, which many of us mistake for our purpose. But uncovering and following our purpose can increase our overall happiness in a way achieving our goals can't. Sometimes it helps to journey through another's story. Allow me to share my own.

As a child, I was ill and given a second chance at life. This profound experience led me to believe that I was indebted to humanity, that I must pay back this invaluable gift through a life of selfless service. Such was the weight of this obligation that it drove my career choices. I explored professions I believed would allow me to "give back" the most—social work, nursing, and personal care for paralyzed patients.

However, there was a palpable disconnect. Despite believing these seemingly altruistic career choices were necessary to be fulfilled, I could never really embrace the thought of actually doing them. I valued the feeling of success, and all that brought with it, and I couldn't reconcile this desire with what I thought should be my purpose. As I explored opportunities, fulfillment eluded me. I was playing multiple roles—supporting my family, being a mother, wife, daughter, and friend—and yet, a void persisted. A piece of the puzzle was missing.

It took a hard, introspective look at myself to unearth the crux of the issue. In the crossroads between what I believed I should be doing and what my heart truly desired, I found my purpose. It wasn't about fitting into a preconceived notion of service, it was about aligning my strengths, values, and passions. This epiphany changed everything.

Transitioning into the role of an executive search consultant, I reveled in the deep, transformative conversations and relationships I forged. It was here, in the realm of coaching—then an emerging field—that I found my true calling. As clients confided in me, discussing their ambitions, fears, and interpersonal challenges, I realized my genuine purpose was facilitating these moments of enlightenment. Observing someone transition from a state of uncertainty to exuding confidence, witnessing their aha moments—that was my purpose.

As we embark on the journey to uncover our purpose, it's important to recognize that the end goal may not always mean a radical change in direction. Sometimes the path you're already on is your purpose, and that's perfectly okay. Let's consider Kendra's journey.

Kendra was a top-performing student who graduated as the valedictorian from a prestigious university, while also playing on the volleyball team, running track, volunteering, and working on the school paper. You're getting the picture—she was a classic high achiever. Despite the economic challenges of the subprime crisis and graduating amid financial turmoil, Kendra received multiple job offers. Drawn by the idea of serving humanity and leveraging her unparalleled problem-solving skills, she chose a high-profile role in law enforcement. But to her surprise, it didn't resonate with her. She took another leap, heading back to school to pursue environmentalism. Ascending rapidly through the ranks, she found herself in executive leadership. A change of leadership left her looking for a new high-profile opportunity.

Our coaching sessions transitioned from leadership development to purpose discovery. Through intense introspection, Kendra realized that her true purpose at that stage in her life was to homeschool her daughter, who faced learning challenges. Surprisingly, for a woman with such a high-achieving background, her most fulfilling role was in what society might deem more "ordinary."

It's pivotal to note that in an era where media glorifies exceptional lives and milestones, purpose isn't always about grandeur. Often, purpose is derived from simple acts that align with our core values and passions. Statistically, many individuals find fulfillment in roles that might not be high-profile or headline-grabbing but provide profound personal satisfaction.

The key may lie in redefining "extraordinary." Perhaps the truly extraordinary life is one where we find joy in the ordinary, relish simple moments, and cherish the vulnerability that makes us human. It's time to shift the focus from the unrelenting pursuit of perfection to the embrace of authenticity and self-acceptance.

Finding one's purpose isn't necessarily about monumental undertakings like curing cancer or saving the whales. It's far more profound and personal than that. Identifying your purpose starts with understanding your core values. By acknowledging what you genuinely value, you can determine who you truly are and what you desire more of in your life. When you align your everyday actions and decisions with these values, you naturally gravitate toward a purpose that resonates with your authentic self. This alignment allows you to discern what you want more of and what you wish to reduce or eliminate from your life.

Moreover, purpose isn't solely tied to our careers. Case in point, Sandy, a chief marketing officer at a major law firm. While her position was undeniably impactful, it wasn't where she found her true purpose. That spark ignited when she taught law students marketing strategies, reveling in the moments of understanding and growth she facilitated for them. Her day job and her purpose were distinct, yet both essential facets of her identity.

Understanding that purpose might not always manifest in the form you expect, or in grand revelations, is empowering.

It's a gentle reminder that it's not about the grandeur of the task but the depth of its alignment with your core. As you reflect on your own journey, remember that sometimes your purpose is hidden in plain sight. Feeling eager to discover yours? Let's delve into the transformative steps ahead. But first, embarking on the journey to discover your true purpose is deeply personal and transformative.

As with any meaningful voyage, there are a few guidelines that can pave the way for a smoother and more enlightening experience:

- Find a calm setting where you won't be interrupted.
- Be kind to yourself as you go through this process.
- Be patient and don't rush the process.
- Don't judge what comes up (there are no wrong answers).
- Values aren't good or bad.
- Stay open to what you discover.
- Understand that a purpose can change over time.

The journey to self-actualization is transformative, taking us on a deep dive into our own psyche and aligning us with our true purpose. But as we explore our inner depths, we might unveil hidden emotions or past experiences that evoke feelings of anxiety or even depression. Dr. Carl Rogers, a renowned psychologist, once said, "The good life is a process, not a state of being. It is a direction, not a destination."[31] The path to discovering one's genuine self might surface feelings of discomfort as we try to reconcile our present with our envisioned ideal. This journey is about looking ahead, focused on future potentials, not dwelling on past regrets. It's not a place for the "should've, could've, would've" mindset, but rather a recognition of our capacity to evolve and step closer to our true selves. As we tread this path, challenges might arise, but it underscores our commitment to a more purposeful, intentional life. Though the path may present its set of hurdles, it's our unwavering commitment to a richer, more intentional life.

Note: If this work leads to feelings of extreme overwhelm, please consult a mental health professional.

STEPS TO FINDING YOUR PURPOSE

IDENTIFYING VALUES: THE BEDROCK OF PURPOSE

For high achievers looking to find and define their purpose, the starting point isn't an ambitious goal or a grand vision. Instead, it begins with something deeply personal and foundational: your values.

At their core, values are the beliefs, principles, and standards that underpin our attitudes and actions. They are the internal compasses that guide us, informing our decisions and influencing our behavior. Values are the nonnegotiables, the lines we draw in the sand of life that demarcate what we stand for and what we won't tolerate. Whether it's integrity, family, ambition, or community, our values are the fundamental essence of who we are and, consequently, are critical in our journey to discover our purpose.

However, the complexities of life mean that sometimes, whether due to external pressures or circumstances, we find ourselves in positions where our values are tested or compromised. It's essential to recognize that in some situations, compromising might be unavoidable. Yet every time we do, it may come at a cost—be it emotional, mental, or even physical. Hence, the clearer we are about what our values are, the more consciously we can navigate these dilemmas.

As my father astutely observed and frequently reminded me, "A value isn't a value if you give it up too easily." His words resonate deeply, emphasizing the importance of steadfastness. In the quest for purpose, identifying and adhering to our values not only defines our journey but also shapes the essence of the legacy we leave behind. His words echoed in my mind when I was offered a position at a private equity firm—a large one. The compensation package would have had a huge impact on my and my husband's future. I started down the path of considering it, but I knew the firm had a reputation of being ruthless and not treating people with respect. In doing my due diligence, I heard of stories, several, where people were brought to tears in meetings as a result of the almost bully behavior that was accepted. Respect has always been an important value of mine, and in the end, I wasn't willing to witness the disrespect of others. I wasn't willing to compromise. If I needed the job or the job was going to advance my goals, I may have compromised, but being clear on your values allows you to make intentional choices.

Finding Your Values

- The following is a long but not exhaustive list of values. Add any that you feel are missing.
- Read the following list of values.
- Cross off the ones that don't seem important to you.
- Review the remaining values and mark the ones that truly resonate with you.
- Continue to repeat this process until you've narrowed down the list to five.
- Rank your top five values.

Accomplishment	Creativity	Health	Punctuality
Accountability	Curiosity	Honesty	Recognition
Accuracy	Dependability	Humor	Relaxation
Adventure	Determination	Imagination	Reliability
Affection	Directness	Impact	Resourcefulness
Affluence	Discipline	Independence	Respect
Altruism	Diversity	Integrity	Security
Ambition	Efficiency	Intelligence	Sensitivity
Assertiveness	Empathy	Justice	Significance
Balance	Enthusiasm	Kindness	Sincerity
Bravery	Excellence	Knowledge	Speed
Calmness	Experience	Leadership	Spirituality
Celebrity	Expertise	Learning	Spontaneity
Challenge	Fairness	Love	Stability
Charity	Faith	Loyalty	Strength
Clarity	Fame	Mindfulness	Success
Comfort	Family	Optimism	Sympathy
Commitment	Fidelity	Originality	Teamwork
Compassion	Flexibility	Passion	Understanding
Completion	Fun	Peace	Vision
Contentment	Generosity	Perfection	Wealth
Control	Grace	Power	Winning

List your top five values here and rank them:

1. ....

2. ....

3. ....

4. ....

5. ....

The words you selected are important because they mean something specific to you. It's important to be clear about exactly what these words mean to you, as sometimes people have different interpretations of the same word. Since the words you chose resonate with you, you likely have a strong association with a way of describing them that is both personal and powerful to you.

Write a short description of what each value means to you.

....

....

....

....

....

Next, ask yourself these questions:

- Why are these values important to me?

- When am I most aligned with my values?

- Am I living authentically according to them?

- Am I straying from them?

Select the value that you feel is most out of alignment and most critical to your happiness and success:

- Write out that value and post it where you will see it often.

- Focus on this value for the next twenty-one days (the time needed to create a new habit).

- Each day, reflect on how you might employ that value in what you are doing. Just the act of having that value present in your mind each day will allow your subconscious to do some of the work for you as you seek new ways to be in alignment.

IDENTIFY PASSION AND FLOW: KEYS TO UNLOCKING YOUR PURPOSE

Once you know your values, the next step in discovering your purpose is to acknowledge your passions. One profound step in the quest to discover your purpose is recognizing and embracing your passions. But what exactly is passion? At its core, passion is an intense desire or enthusiasm for something. It's that fire in your belly, the thing that excites you, that you can spend hours on without feeling the weight of time. Passion is the energy that fills you with joy, curiosity, and a sense of deep fulfillment.

Closely intertwined with passion is the concept of "flow," a term popularized by psychologist Mihaly Csikszentmihalyi.[32] He termed *flow* as that state of being where you are so immersed in an activity that the world around you seems to vanish. Time becomes distorted, self-consciousness disappears, and all that remains is you and the task at hand. It's when your skills align perfectly with the challenge, leading to an elevated state of concentration and engagement.

So, why are passion and flow so vital in the journey to find your purpose? Well, **activities or pursuits that ignite your passion and induce flow are clear indicators of what truly resonates with your intrinsic self.** These are activities you don't just do, you feel them deeply. They reflect aspects of who you are and what brings meaning to your life. And when you find your passion and flow, you gain valuable insights into your true purpose.

Reflecting and inquiring can illuminate desires, interests, and aspirations that might have been overshadowed by daily routines or external pressures. Whether it's a particular activity, feeling, relationship, or experience, identifying what you genuinely crave can be a telling signpost pointing toward your deeper passions and, by extension, your purpose.

For the next exercise, record your thoughts in a journal. As we've discussed, writing down thoughts leads to deeper understanding and clarity. Writing the answers to the following questions is a record to help you look for patterns and commonalities and gain perspective on what brings you closer to your purpose:

- What activities make me lose track of time?
- What topics or subjects can I spend hours talking about without getting bored?
- When do I feel the most alive and energized? What am I doing during these moments?
- Which projects or tasks do I gravitate toward, even when they're not assigned to me?
- What dreams or goals have persisted since childhood?
- What causes or issues deeply resonate with me?
- If money and time were not constraints, what would I do?
- Which activities make me feel like the best version of myself?
- What do I frequently daydream about?
- When have I felt the proudest or most fulfilled? What was I doing during those times?
- What do I love to read, watch, or learn about in my free time?
- Who are my role models, and why do I admire them? What aspects of their lives or careers are appealing?

- If I could teach a class on any topic, what would it be?
- What have I accomplished that I feel great about?
- What tasks or hobbies do I voluntarily engage in without expecting any external rewards?

Review your responses. Do you see a connection or pattern among the answers? Were there any surprises? What did you learn about yourself? What ways can you integrate your passions into your day-to-day activities and connect them with your goals?

PURPOSE THROUGH RESEARCH: EXPLORATION AND UNEXPECTED LESSONS

When on the quest to find purpose, exploration is pivotal. But sometimes the paths we investigate might not align with our initial expectations, and that's okay.

I've always felt this drive to blend my business acumen with a profound need to serve humanity. The not-for-profit sector appeared to be the perfect marriage of these two worlds. Eager to understand the landscape, I reached out to five senior leaders within the space, inviting them for a meal. Four responded positively to a lunch invitation, and one opted for dinner. That dinner turned into a comically memorable evening when my guest enjoyed her wine a little too much. We had a very "spirited" discussion before I had to put her in a taxi at the end of the meal!

While the evening had its lighter moments, the insights I garnered from these meetings were invaluable, albeit not entirely optimistic. Most of these leaders, despite working for noble causes, didn't feel the direct impact of their good work daily. They found themselves navigating organizational politics, relentless fundraising drives, and the challenges of collaborating with volunteer board members who didn't always grasp the intricacies of their operations. The big picture, the very impact on individuals they sought to help, often got lost in the minutiae. Recognizing this disconnect, I decided to explore different avenues to serve my purpose.

Researching and seeking insights from those entrenched in your fields of interest can offer invaluable perspective. Take a friend of mine as another example. She had been a banker since her graduation. However, during her own introspective journey, she uncovered a dormant passion for acting. Instead of dismissing this revelation, she chased it. She enrolled in acting classes and dedicated her free hours to engaging with instructors, absorbing all she could. Soon, she realized her dream wasn't just a whimsical fantasy, it was attainable. In a stroke of beginner's luck, she landed a role in a movie on her first audition! Sure, there were rejections that followed, but her initial success was a testament to the power of exploration and persistence.

The lesson here is twofold: First, research is crucial. Investigate the areas you're passionate about. And remain open to the journey. It's exploratory in nature. One avenue might lead to another, and sometimes, the path you initially thought was yours might pivot into something even more resonant. Remember, the objective isn't just to find a purpose but to find one that genuinely aligns with your core.

TAPPING INTO THE UNCONSCIOUS: A DEEP DIVE INTO SELF

One invaluable step in the journey to finding purpose involves delving deep into the realms of the unconscious mind. The unconscious mind, a concept rooted in psychology, is a reservoir of feelings, thoughts, urges, and memories that are outside of our conscious awareness. It's a vast space, storing past experiences and feelings, and it can influence our behavior in ways we don't readily recognize. The key to harnessing its wisdom lies in accessing and understanding its contents. Mindfulness and meditation are the keys to reaching that level of conscious awareness.

THE SPIRITUAL PATH TO PURPOSE

For believers and nonbelievers alike, faith is an important part of purpose.

Faith for the Believer. If you believe in God, Jesus, or any higher power, start by grounding yourself in prayer or meditation. Ask for guidance, clarity, and signs that will direct you toward your purpose. Ask how you can serve. As you pray, be open to receiving messages, even if they don't come immediately or in ways you expect. Sometimes answers can be subtle, found in the rhythm of daily life, a chance conversation, or an unexpected event. Your faith can serve as your compass, aligning you with the divine plan that's been set for you.

Faith for the Non-Believer: Even if you don't believe in a deity, the concept of faith can still be significant. Think of faith as trust—trust in the journey, in the universe, and most importantly, in yourself. Consider the internal nudges, intuitions, and gut feelings you experience as "the knowing within us," guiding you toward your path. When seeking clarity, take a moment to sit silently, breathe deeply, and tune into these inner messages.

The Power of Shared Faith: I've personally experienced the magic of shared faith with my dear friend, Kathryn. Whenever faced with a dilemma or in search of clarity, we come together—often over a simple phone call—to ask the spirit for guidance. We sit in quiet reflection, sometimes for minutes, sometimes longer, waiting for a sign or a message. Whether one comes or not, the act itself brings solace and a strengthened sense of direction.

Embrace faith with an open heart, and let it gently guide you closer to your true purpose. After all, in the words of Martin Luther King Jr., "Faith is taking the first step even when you don't see the whole staircase."

THE GROWTH MINDSET: A KEY TO UNLOCKING PURPOSE

At the intersection of self-awareness and potential lies the concept of a growth mindset. Coined by Dr. Carol Dweck, this idea has transformed the way many perceive challenges, abilities, and ultimately, their life's purpose. But how can this mindset be a catalyst in your journey toward discovering purpose?

When you operate from a space of growth, you inherently believe that no challenge is too big or no skill too alien to master. Understanding and embracing your strengths is a part of this journey. However, the magic lies in your belief in self-evolution. Throughout my experiences, I've witnessed countless individuals unearth and hone skills they didn't initially possess, solely fueled by their purpose and the mindset that they can grow.

JOURNEYING TOWARD PURPOSE

Discovering purpose is a life-changing journey, one I genuinely hope you embrace every step of. By intertwining elements like identifying core values, recognizing passions, tapping into spirituality, and employing mindfulness, you create a rich tapestry of experiences and insights. Coupled with a growth mindset, the path to purpose becomes not only clearer but also more fulfilling.

REFLECTION

- **Acknowledge Your Current Mindset**: Begin by understanding where you currently stand. Are you more inclined toward a fixed or growth mindset?

- **Challenge Your Beliefs**: Ask yourself: Do I believe talents are innate? When faced with a setback, do I see it as a limitation or a lesson?

- **Recognize the Power of Yet**: Instead of saying, "I can't do this," add a simple "yet" at the end. This changes the narrative to "I can't do this yet," emphasizing the potential for growth.

- **Visualize Growth**: Reflect on moments in your past when you developed a new skill or improved an existing one. How did it feel? How did you achieve it?

- **Affirm Your Growth Potential**: Continuously remind yourself: "I am capable of growth. I can learn. I can evolve."

- **Embrace Challenges**: Instead of avoiding difficulties, see them as opportunities to stretch your abilities and learn. They are the best teachers.

CHAPTER 8:
CONCLUSION–SOARING HIGH

Hey there, High Achiever! Let's warmly embrace the insights we've uncovered and eagerly anticipate the further depths of understanding that beckon.

From our initial encounters, the pathway of a high-achieving woman unfurled as both challenging and deeply rewarding. Every chapter, every revelation, has been an invitation to introspection. With the stress-management strategies we've shared, you're poised to navigate life's challenges with both strength and serenity. Remember, it's not about circumventing obstacles but about embracing and growing from them with grace.

Together, we delved deep into the essence of who you are, unraveling layers: the subtle undertones of impostor syndrome, the transformative journey from uncertainty to clarity, and the multifaceted world of relationships. Here's a comforting truth: these experiences, these introspections, resonate universally. **Every individual encounters moments of doubt and discovery, but now you're better equipped to move through them with wisdom and understanding.**

Diving into the realm of relationships and understanding varied personalities, consider each connection as a mirror, reflecting parts of ourselves and teaching us valuable lessons. Value these reflections, grow from these encounters, and as you continue on, lift and be lifted. For our endeavors are not just about personal growth but about enriching and being enriched by the tapestry of lives around us.

Centered in our explorations was the quest for a deeper purpose. Beyond accomplishments and milestones, it's the profound *why* that infuses our efforts with meaning. This purpose, your inner compass, ensures every step you take is resonant and purposeful.

May your path be illuminated with purpose, passion, and the warmth of shared discovery. With your newfound insights and ever-present grace, may you continue to inspire and be inspired. You possess the wisdom, the heart, and an expansive future brimming with possibilities. The next chapter of your life, rich with promise, awaits.

Continue with heart.
Delve with purpose.
Shine your unique light.

Barbara

You can find me at
barbara@elevateorganizations.com
https://www.elevateorganizations.com

ACKNOWLEDGMENTS

This book, a labor of love and determination, would not have seen the light of day without the unwavering support and contributions of many remarkable individuals.

Firstly, my heartfelt gratitude goes to Holly Crawshaw. Holly, your initial writing efforts were instrumental in bringing this project to life. Your belief in the importance of my message and your constant encouragement were the wind beneath the wings of this endeavor. Even though I took on a significant portion of the writing, your foundational work and faith in the worth of my words were invaluable.

To my astute and dedicated editors, Kelly Lamb and Christine Stock of Soul Seed Legacy, your keen eyes and professional touch have sculpted and refined this manuscript into something far greater than I could have achieved alone. Your guidance through the intricate maze of the publishing world has been nothing short of a masterclass.

A special acknowledgment is owed to Sabrina Greer of Soul Seed Legacy. Sabrina, your expertise and the resources of your team have been a cornerstone in the journey of this book. The analogy of helping to "birth the baby" could not be more apt, and I am eternally grateful for your role in bringing this "baby" to fruition.

I extend my profound thanks to the wonderful women who took the time to read and review the manuscript before its publication: Krista Webster, Simone Hughes, Aleena Mazhar, Amanda Shuchat, and Andrea Clayton. Each of you has not only contributed to the betterment of this book, but you have also been a source of personal inspiration over the years. Your individual successes and journeys have taught me invaluable lessons, shaping the pages of this book as well as my perspective and growth.

This book is not just a collection of pages but a tapestry woven from the contributions, insights, and support of each one of you. Thank you for being part of this remarkable journey.

WORKS CITED

1. National Library of Medicine, "Francis Galton" https://www.ncbi.nlm.nih.gov/pmc/articles/PMC4590158/ Accessed October 30, 2023

2. National Library of Medicine, "Nature vs. Nurture" https://www.ncbi.nlm.nih.gov/pmc/articles/PMC3119494/ Accessed October 30, 2023

3. American Psychological Association, "Children use wealth cues to evaluate others" https://psycnet.apa.org/record/2016-11562-001 Accessed October 30, 2023

4. National Library of Medicine, "Hans Selye (1907–1982): Founder of the stress theory" https://www.ncbi.nlm.nih.gov/pmc/articles/PMC5915631/ Accessed October 30, 2023

5. American Psychological Association, "Stress" https://www.apa.org/topics/stress
Accessed November 21, 2023

6. The Wellbeing Project, Rick Hanson. https://wellbeing-project.org/rick-hanson/ Accessed October 30, 2023

7. The Dynamic Neural Retraining System™, https://retrainingthebrain.com/ Accessed October 30, 2023

8. Loder, Vanessa. "Can Stress Kill You? Research Says Only If You Believe It Can." Forbes. June 3, 2015. https://www.forbes.com/sites/vanessaloder/2015/06/03/can-stress-kill-you-research-says-only-if-you-believe-it-can/?sh=2e3d9d3f682e Accessed November 21, 2023

9. National Library of Medicine, "Acute stress enhances adult rat hippocampal neurogenesis and activation of newborn neurons via secreted astrocytic FGF2" https://www.ncbi.nlm.nih.gov/pmc/articles/PMC3628086/ Accessed October 30, 2023

10. National Library of Medicine, "Inflammation: The Common Pathway of Stress-Related Diseases" https://www.ncbi.nlm.nih.gov/pmc/articles/PMC5476783/. Accessed October 30, 2023

11. Schechter, David. *The MindBody Workbook*, November 1999, Mindbody Medicine Publications

12. American Psychological Association, "Psychological vulnerability and stress: The effects of self-affirmation on sympathetic nervous system responses to naturalistic stressors" https://psycnet.apa.org/record/2009-14439-006 Accessed December 12, 2023

13. Sage Journals, "Self-Affirmations Provide a Broader Perspective on Self-Threat" https://journals.sagepub.com/doi/abs/10.1177/0146167214554956 Accessed December 12, 2023

14. Amen Clinics, "The Number One Habit To Develop In Order To Feel More Positive" https://www.amenclinics.com/blog/number-one-habit-develop-order-feel-positive/ Accessed December 12, 2023

15. Healthline, "How to Hack Your Hormones for a Better Mood" https://www.healthline.com/health/happy-hormone Accessed October 30, 2023

16. Mayo Clinic, "Stress Relief from Laughter? It's No Joke" https://www.mayoclinic.org/healthy-lifestyle/stress-management/in-depth/stress-relief/art-20044456 Accessed October 30, 2023

17. World Health Organization, "Burn-out an 'occupational phenomenon': International Classification of Diseases" https://www.who.int/news/item/28-05-2019-burn-out-an-occupational-phenomenon-international-classification-of-diseases Accessed October 30, 2023

18. Monster.com, "Dangerously Stressful Work Environments Force Workers to Seek New Employment" https://www.monster.com/about/a/dangerously-stressful-work-environments-force-workers-to-seek-new-empl4162014-d3126696 Accessed October 30, 2023

19. American Psychological Association, "The American workforce faces compounding pressure" https://www.apa.org/pubs/reports/work-well-being/compounding-pressure-2021
Accessed October 30, 2023

20. Statistica, https://www.statista.com/topics/1265/magazines/ Accessed October 30, 2023

21. National Library of Medicine, "Body Dissatisfaction, Importance of Appearance, and Body Appreciation in Men and Women Over the Lifespan" https://www.ncbi.nlm.nih.gov/pmc/articles/PMC6928134/ Accessed October 30, 2023

22. American Psychological Association, "What is Cognitive Behavioral Therapy?" https://www.apa.org/ptsd-guideline/patients-and-families/cognitive-behavioral Accessed October 30, 2023

23. Journal of Social and Personal Relationships, https://journals.sagepub.com/home/SPR Accessed November 22, 2023

24. TED Talk, Amy Cuddy, "Your Body Language May Shape Who You Are." June 2012. https://www.ted.com/talks/amy_cuddy_your_body_language_may_shape_who_you_are?language=en Accessed October 30, 2023

25. Harvard Business School. "Why Emotional Intelligence Is Important in Leadership." https://online.hbs.edu/blog/post/emotional-intelligence-in-leadership Accessed December 12, 2023

26. Dr. Dan Siegel, https://drdansiegel.com/ Accessed October 30, 2023

27. The Society of Analytical Psychology, https://www.thesap.org.uk/articles-on-jungian-psychology-2/carl-gustav-jung/ Accessed October 30, 2023

28. Clark, Courtney. *The Successful Struggle: Powerful Techniques to Achieve Accelerated Resilience*, February 2016, Incline Ink

29. Duckworth, Angela. *Grit: The Power of Passion and Perseverance*, January 2016, Scribner

30. *Live to 100: Secrets of the Blue Zones,* Netflix, 2023

31. Simply Psychology, Carl Rogers. https://www.simplypsychology.org/carl-rogers.html
Accessed October 30, 2023

32. Csikszentmihalyi, Mihaly, *Flow: The Psychology of Optimal Experience*, July 2008, HarperCollins

Made in the USA
Middletown, DE
15 May 2024

54258112R00117